
This journal is abstracted or indexed in: *Academic Abstracts*; *Contents Pages in Education; Education Index; Education Abstracts; ISI: Current Contents/Social & Behavioral Sciences, Social Sciences Citation Index, Research Alert, Social Science*; and *PsycINFO/Psychological Abstracts*. Microform copies of this journal are available through Bell & Howell Information and Learning, P. O. Box 1346, Ann Arbor, MI 48106–1346. For more information, call 1-800-521-0600 x2888.

First published 2002 by Lawrence Erlbaum Associates, Inc.

Published 2019 by Routledge
2 Park Square, Milton Park, Abingdon, Oxon OX14 4RN
52 Vanderbilt Avenue, New York, NY 10017

Routledge is an imprint of the Taylor & Francis Group, an informa business

ISBN 13: 978-0-8058-9670-1 (pbk)

ISSN 0046–1520

Educational Psychologist

Official Publication of the
Division of Educational Psychology of the
American Psychological Association

Volume 37, Number 1, Winter 2002

EDUCATIONAL PSYCHOLOGIST, *37*(1), 1–3

Introduction: Using Qualitative Methods to Enrich Understandings of Self-Regulated Learning

Nancy E. Perry
Department of Educational and Counseling Psychology and Special Education
University of British Columbia

The articles appearing in this special issue of the *Educational Psychologist* were originally presented in a symposium at the annual conference of the *American Educational Research Association* (April, 2000). They reflect a growing interest among "students" of self-regulated learning in finding ways to study this phenomenon in real contexts and real time, in events rather than as aptitudes (Winne & Perry, 2000). Theorists have used the term *self-regulated learning* (SRL) to describe independent, academically effective forms of learning that involve metacognition, intrinsic motivation, and strategic action (Winne & Perry, 2000; Zimmerman, 1990). The preponderance of research over the past quarter century has measured SRL as an aptitude. Traditionally, aptitudes have been defined as in person, across situation characteristics—relatively enduring attributes of an individual that can be aggregated over or abstracted from behavior across multiple events (Winne & Perry, 2000, p. 534). Predominantly, investigations of SRL relied on survey methods to assess students' self-reports of actions generalized across settings and situations (e.g., students are asked to indicate what strategies they typically use to prepare for tests or do academic work).

These investigations have revealed many facets of SRL (e.g., learners' ability to analyze task parameters, monitor progress toward an end goal, and apply effective strategies to keep them on course), how they relate to one another, and how they relate to outcomes we value (e.g., successful task completion). However, they do not reveal what learners actually do, versus what they say they do, or how features of a particular learning context can influence what learners generally think and do. Investigations of SRL in events address these limitations by providing opportunities to take snapshots of students' actions embedded in a larger, longer series of situations that unfold over time.

Requests for reprints should be sent to Nancy E. Perry, Department of Educational and Counseling Psychology and Special Education, University of British Columbia, 2125 Main Mall, Vancouver, B.C. V6T 1Z4. E-mail: nancy.perry@ubc.ca

Increasingly, SRL theorists and researchers are emphasizing the need for research in educational psychology in general, and SRL in particular, to attend to the role of context in shaping students' cognitions and motivations (Anderman & Anderman, 2000; Pintrich, 1994). This emphasis accompanies the growing interest in sociocognitive, socioconstructivist, and sociocultural theories of learning, and the realization that, to be ecologically valid and practically relevant, our research must broaden its focus to reflect individuals acting within psychological, disciplinary, social, and cultural contexts (Goodenow, 1992; Solomon, 1995). This new emphasis has implications for how we study phenomena such as SRL and prompts reconsideration of traditional distinctions between aptitudes for SRL in and across events (Stanford Aptitude Seminar, 2001). Sociotheories prompt investigations of SRL in naturalistic contexts using methods and measures that can be adapted by researchers and teachers to suit the unique characteristics of a particular teaching and learning environment (Paris & Paris, 2001; Randi & Corno, 2000). Such measures are intended to capture students recognizing specific opportunities to engage in SRL (e.g., a student expresses, "Wow, this is hard," while working on a math problem) and then exercising SRL in that situation (e.g., the student takes out a piece of paper to make a table that reflects aspects of the problem). Also, such measures are intended to capture the extent to which students' aptitudes for SRL differ across settings and situations. Designing such measures requires that researchers consider aptitudes for SRL as in-person, in-situation characteristics and ask questions such as the following:

- What data can represent SRL in events?
- What properties do different kinds of data have and how should these influence decisions about gathering and analyzing data?
- What are the relative strengths and weaknesses of different kinds of data and how are these best balanced in relation to topics that researchers might wish to investigate? (adapted from Winne, Jamieson-Noel, & Muis, in press)

The researchers contributing to this special issue are grappling with these questions. In their programs of research, they have combined quantitative and qualitative methods and measured SRL in and across events. However, for this issue, I asked them to highlight one or two of the qualitative methods they use to support in-depth, *in situ* investigations of SRL. In addition, I asked them to describe how the methods they chose to highlight elaborate or challenge understandings of particular facets of SRL. The result is a group of articles that demonstrates the potential qualitative methods have for enriching understandings about how students perceive particular teaching–learning contexts and how their perceptions influence their beliefs about themselves as learners, the learning process, and the decisions they make about how to regulate their behavior in school (Perry, VandeKamp, Mercer, & Nordby, 2002). In addition, the authors of articles in this issue articulate how different methods can reveal multiple aspects of SRL, and provide opportunities for researchers to consider evidence concerning SRL from many different perspectives (Patrick & Middleton, 2002).

OVERVIEW OF ARTICLES IN THIS ISSUE

Perry et al. (2002) described how they use observations, in the form of running records, to examine what teachers do and say to support young children's metacognition, intrinsic motivation, and strategic action during reading and writing activities. Specifically, they have developed a three-part observation protocol that applies both conceptual and analytic coding categories to characterize classroom reading and writing tasks, authority structures, and evaluation practices that either promote or curtail children's development of and engagement in SRL. Their observations provide evidence of students in kindergarten through Grade 3 regulating their behavior (e.g., planning, monitoring, problem solving) during complex, multifaceted reading and writing tasks (e.g., writing a research report). Also, their observations indicate young children can have much more differentiated motivational profiles than much of the survey research has suggested (Paris & Newman, 1990).

Similarly, Meyer and Turner (2002) described how they use discourse analysis to examine the influence of teachers' talk and actions on upper elementary students' motivation and self-regulation in mathematics classrooms. Specifically, they have analyzed transcripts of whole class mathematics lessons and developed a set of coding categories that characterize scaffolded and nonscaffolded instruction and the kinds of discourse that accompany them. In classrooms where scaffolded discourse is present, teachers ask students to engage in self-talk that models (for their peers, or their teacher) their approach to solving mathematical problems. Teachers offer guiding statements to support students' development of problem-solving strategies, and they ask questions that check students' understandings of mathematical concepts. When scaffolded discourse is present in classrooms, Meyer and Turner indicate that students and teachers are engaged in *co-regulation* (McCaslin & Good, 1996). In contrast, in classrooms where nonscaffolded instruction predominates, the discourse includes a lot of teacher directives, and student involvement is very limited.

Patrick and Middleton (2002) described how they use observations and interviews to examine middle school students' cognitive, metacognitive, motivational, and collaborative engagement in Project-Based Science (PBS; Blumenfeld, Marx, Patrick, Krajcik, & Soloway, 1997). Consistent with socioconstructivist theories of learning, this approach to science instruction asks students to generate "driving" questions and then work collaboratively to design investigations that will answer them. Patrick and Middleton emphasized the value of using both observations and interviews to provide "rich and contextualized" descriptions of students' SRL in PBS. Also, they emphasized the value of using multiple methods to triangulate research findings and capture the complexity of the SRL construct.

DeGroot (2002) described her use of unstructured in-depth, structured, and semistructured interview protocols to examine how interpersonal relationships and school or class policies and practices can help or hinder high school students' motivation, self-regulation, and achievement. Specifically, she drew examples from interviews with students and teachers across three different studies, each one using a different interview protocol. Each application highlights the power of using interviews to study the intra- and interindividual properties of SRL. Particularly, DeGroot stressed the value of examining the words students and teachers use to describe complex educational phenomena, such as SRL. Also, she outlined the challenges inherent in using interviews to study motivation and self-regulation.

Finally, Reed, Schallert, and Deithloff (2002) described how they combine the Experience Sampling Method (ESM), developed by Csikszentmihalyi and Larson (1987), and retrospective questionnaires to study college students' involvement in writing activities. They use ESM to capture the "phase change" in a task when self-regulatory processes give way to "nonself-focused" involvement with a task. Their investigations indicate that self-regulation, which seems antithetical to the "flow" state associated with total immersion in a task, may actually be a stimulus that uses volitional strategies to move learners from a self-focused state to an involvement in the task state.

In addition to their use of qualitative methods to study SRL in events, several other themes tie the articles in this issue together. First, each article attends to relations between context and behavior. Second, each article attempts to study SRL, or some facet of it, as it occurs in real contexts and real time. Finally, taken together, the articles offer perspectives on SRL across disciplines (e.g., reading, writing, math, and science), and across a wide developmental trajectory, from kindergarten through college. Butler's (2002) commentary cuts across articles, elaborating these themes, highlighting how the programs of research described in these articles are enriching understandings of SRL, and articulating conceptual and methodological problems that remain for students of SRL to solve.

REFERENCES

Anderman, L. H., & Anderman, E. M. (2000). Considering contexts in educational psychology: Introduction to the special issue. *Educational Psychologist, 35,* 67–68.

Blumenfeld, P. C., Marx, R. W., Patrick, H., Krajcik, J. S., & Soloway, E. (1997). Teaching for understanding. In B. J. Biddle, T. L. Good, & I. F. Goodson (Eds.), *International handbook of teachers and teaching. Volume II* (pp. 819–878). Dordrecht, The Netherlands: Kluwer Academic.

Butler, D. L. (2002). Qualitative approaches to investigating self-regulated learning: Contributions and challenges. *Educational Psychologist, 37,* 59–63.

Csikszentmihalyi, M., & Larson, R. (1987). Validity and reliability of the Experience Sampling Method. *The Journal of Nervous and Mental Disease, 175,* 526–536.

DeGroot, E. V. (2002). Learning through interviewing: Students and teachers talk about learning and schooling. *Educational Psychologist, 37,* 47–58.

Goodenow, C. (1992). Strengthening the links between educational psychology and the study of social contexts. *Educational Psychologist, 27,* 177–196.

McCaslin, M., & Good, T. L. (1996). The informal curriculum. In D. C. Berliner & R. C. Calfee (Eds.), *Handbook of educational psychology* (pp. 622–670). New York: Simon & Schuster.

Meyer, D. K., & Turner, J. C. (2002). Using instructional discourse analysis to study scaffolding of student self-regulation. *Educational Psychologist, 37,* 5–13.

Paris, S. G., & Newman, R. S. (1990). Developmental aspects of self-regulated learning. *Educational Psychologist, 25,* 87–102.

Paris, S. G., & Paris, A. H. (2001). Classroom applications of research on self-regulated learning. *Educational Psychologist, 36,* 89–101.

Patrick, H., & Middleton, M. J. (2002). Turning the kaleidoscope: What we see when self-regulated learning is viewed with a qualitative lens. *Educational Psychologist, 37,* 27–39.

Perry, N. E., VandeKamp, K. O., Mercer, L. K., & Nordby, C. J. (2002). Investigating student-teacher interactions that foster self-regulated learning. *Educational Psychologist, 37,* 15–25.

Pintrich, P. R. (1994). Continuities and discontinuities: Future directions for research in educational psychology. *Educational Psychologist, 29,* 137–148.

Randi, J., & Corno, L. (2000). Teacher innovations in self-regulated learning. In P. Pintrich, M. Boekaerts, & M. Zeidner (Eds.), *Handbook of self-regulation* (pp. 651–685). Orlando, FL: Academic.

Reed, J. H., Schallert, D. L., & Deithloff, L. F. (2002). Investigating the interface between self-regulation and involvement processes. *Educational Psychologist, 37,* 41–45.

Solomon, G. (1995). Reflections on the field of educational psychology by the outgoing journal editor. *Educational Psychologist, 30,* 105–108.

Stanford Aptitude Seminar. (2001). *Remaking the concept of aptitude: Extending the legacy of Richard E. Snow.* Mahwah, NJ: Lawrence Erlbaum Associates, Inc.

Winne, P. H., & Perry, N. E. (2000). Measuring self-regulated learning. In P. Pintrich, M. Boekaerts, & M. Zeidner (Eds.), *Handbook of self-regulation* (pp. 531–566). Orlando, FL: Academic.

Winne, P. H., Jamieson-Noel, D. L., & Muis, K. (in press). Methodological issues and advances in researching tactics, strategies, and self-regulated learning. In M. L. Maehr & P. R. Pintrich (Eds.), *Advances in motivation and achievement* (Vol. 12). Greenwich, CT: JAI.

Zimmerman, B. J. (1990). Self-regulated learning and academic achievement: An overview. *Educational Psychologist, 25,* 3–17.

EDUCATIONAL PSYCHOLOGIST, 37(1), 5–15

Investigating Teacher–Student Interactions That Foster Self-Regulated Learning

Nancy E. Perry, Karen O. VandeKamp, Louise K. Mercer, and Carla J. Nordby
Department of Educational and Counseling Psychology and Special Education
University of British Columbia

This article describes the use of qualitative methods to study young children's engagement in self-regulated learning. In particular, it describes how fine-grained analyses of running records have enabled us to characterize what teachers say and do to foster young children's metacognitive, intrinsically motivated, and strategic behavior during reading and writing activities in their classrooms. This article argues that in-class observations followed by semistructured, retrospective interviews ameliorate many of the difficulties researchers have experienced in past studies of young children's motivation and self-regulation. The observations and interviews provide evidence of children in kindergarten through Grade 3 engaging in self-regulatory behaviors, such as planning, monitoring, problem-solving, and evaluating, during complex reading and writing tasks. Also, they reveal variance in young children's motivational profiles that is more consistent with older students than has heretofore been assumed. Moreover, the *in situ* investigations of young children's self-regulated learning offer important insights into the nature and degree of support young children require to be successfully self-regulating.

In the past quarter century there has been a proliferation of research on self-regulated learning (SRL), a descriptor for independent, academically effective forms of learning that involve metacognition, intrinsic motivation, and strategic action (Winne & Perry, 2000). Much of this research has relied on survey methods to assess students' self-reports of actions generalized across settings and situations. Also, many researchers have used experimental or quasi-experimental designs to assess the impact of interventions on variables associated with SRL. Although these investigations have identified multiple facets of SRL, their interrelationships, and their relations to outcomes educators value (i.e., success in school and beyond), they have not provided a detailed characterization of SRL in *real* contexts and in *real* time.

Recently, interest in sociocognitive and sociocultural models of learning has prompted investigations of SRL in naturalistic settings (e.g., classrooms) and the application of qualitative techniques to support more in-depth and on-line investigations of particular facets of SRL. We believe these approaches have tremendous potential to enrich understandings about how students perceive particular teaching–learning contexts and how these perceptions influence their beliefs about themselves as learners, their goals and expectations, and the decisions they make about how to regulate their behavior in school. For example, observations, in the form of running records, can reflect what learners actually do versus what they recall or believe they do. Also, they allow us to link behaviors of teachers and students to contexts and conditions. Discourse analysis allows a fine-grained analysis of what teachers say to support or curtail students' SRL and how students respond. Finally, semistructured and retrospective interviews that are linked to observations can illuminate aspects of students' behavior that are not readily observable (e.g., metacognitive processes).

Each of these tools has proven useful in our investigations of young children's SRL (Perry, 1998; Perry & VandeKamp, 2000; Perry, VandeKamp, & Hoption, 1999). Whereas the preponderance of theoretical and empirical work concerning academic self-regulation has involved students in the upper elementary grades through college, our research targets students in kindergarten through Grade 3 and challenges long-held views that children under age 10 have difficulties coordinating the complex cognitive and metacognitive processes involved in SRL (Pressley, Forrest-Pressley,

Requests for reprints should be sent to Nancy E. Perry, Department of Educational and Counseling Psychology and Special Education, University of British Columbia, 2125 Main Mall, Vancouver, BC, Canada V6T 1Z4. E-mail: nancy.perry@ubc.ca

Elliott-Faust, & Miller, 1985; Winne, 1995; Zimmerman, 1990). Our observations and interviews provide evidence of young children regulating their behavior (e.g., planning, monitoring, problem-solving, and evaluating) during complex, multifaceted reading and writing tasks (e.g., writing a research report). Moreover, our findings challenge views that young children are protected from motivational orientations that undermine SRL because they tend to hold incremental views of ability, rate their ability highly, and expect to do well as long as they exert effort (Paris & Newman, 1990).

In our investigations, between 25% and 50% of the children we observed and interviewed demonstrated motivational vulnerabilities that have implications for SRL. For example, they exhibited negative affect when offered feedback that pinpointed errors in their work, and they chose easy tasks over challenging tasks that provided opportunities to develop and practice SRL. Finally, our observations and interviews reveal how features of literacy tasks, authority structures, and evaluation practices influence young children's beliefs, values, expectations, and actions concerning reading and writing, and what teachers do and say to promote (or curtail) SRL in their classrooms.

In part, we attribute our success in documenting young children's SRL to our use of qualitative methods that target issues young children value (e.g., learning to read and write), use language they understand (e.g., the language of their classroom), and assess their SRL in the context of naturally occurring literacy events in their classrooms (Cain & Dweck, 1995). In the sections that follow, we provide a brief overview of our program of research and then focus on how we have used observations in the form of running records to enrich our understandings of what teachers do and say to promote young children's SRL.

OVERVIEW OF OUR PROGRAM OF RESEARCH

Our program of research has two main objectives: to identify features of classroom tasks, authority structures, and evaluation practices that support young children's development of independent, academically effective forms of reading and writing, and to work collaboratively with teachers to design literacy activities that contain these features. Over the past 5 years, we have taken a multipronged approach to meeting these objectives. First, we observed in classrooms and characterized them as high or low in promoting SRL. Next, we worked with primary teachers, supporting their efforts to create literacy environments for their students that were "high-SRL." Finally, we went into classrooms to observe teachers' innovations and to document their impact on students' engagement in learning.

Initial Observations in Classrooms

As part of a multiple and embedded case study, Perry (1998) observed literacy activities in five Grade 2 and 3 classrooms. These classrooms were selected from a larger pool of classrooms in a suburban school district in British Columbia. The observations, which took the form of running records, occurred weekly for 6 months (January through June 1995) during regularly scheduled reading and writing activities in the classrooms. Based on these observations, three of the classrooms were characterized as high-SRL classrooms. Teachers in these classrooms engaged students in complex, open-ended reading and writing activities (e.g., "doing" research), offered them choices and opportunities to control challenge in completing those tasks, and provided them with opportunities to evaluate their own and others' work. Also, these teachers provided instrumental support to students, carefully orchestrating instruction to provide students with the domain and strategy knowledge they needed to operate independently, helping them to make appropriate choices, encouraging them to expand their developing abilities by attempting challenging tasks, and using nonthreatening evaluation practices that emphasized personal progress and encouraged students to interpret errors as opportunities to learn.

In contrast, in the two low-SRL classrooms, students were engaged in simple, closed activities, which often focused on specific skills apart from authentic reading and writing (e.g., correcting spelling and punctuation errors in a sentence the teacher wrote on the board). In these activities, students' choices were limited. Challenge and criteria for evaluation were controlled by the teacher and were typically the same for all students. Teachers' support in these classrooms typically targeted the procedural aspects of task completion (e.g., giving directions, distributing materials). In short, there were few opportunities in these classrooms for students to develop or engage in SRL. Therefore, the characteristics of the high-SRL classrooms—what teachers said and did in these classrooms—became the targets for our subsequent work with teachers.

Working With Teachers

Findings from recent research on teacher development indicate that learning to teach in new ways requires opportunities for ongoing reflection, plus support and guidance from peers (Borko & Putnam, 1998). Our project brought teachers together as a community of professionals and provided them with guided and sustained opportunities to collaborate with colleagues. Some teachers have been working with us since April 1997. Palincsar, Magnusson, Morano, Ford, and Brown (1998) characterize communities of teachers as intellectual groups with shared goals and purposes, engaging in collaborative planning, enacting, and reflecting. In these communities, learning proceeds from action, expertise is distributed, and knowledge is socially constructed. Trust among group members is fundamental for functioning as a community, and trust requires a climate in which all views are valued and the cost of errors is small (Lave & Wenger, 1991). In our community, teachers were involved in conversations with us and with one another that prompted them to critically examine their current approaches to literacy assessment and instruction, consider alternatives, and experiment with new teaching and learning strategies in their classrooms.

In the spring of 1997, primary teachers from the same suburban district that was used in Perry's original study were invited to join an action research group with a shared goal to develop tasks and assessments that would reflect "best practices" in early literacy instruction. Our group met for the first time on April 10, 1997, and included 10 primary teachers, 3 school-based remedial–resource teachers, 1 district curriculum consultant, and 2 university researchers (who are also teachers). This group stayed fairly constant through June 1998. In total, we worked with 16 teachers who reflected a range of teaching experience (2–20 years), educational backgrounds, and beliefs about what constitutes effective literacy instruction for young children. In September 1998 through June 1999, we worked with subset of five teachers from the larger group who were particularly interested in and adept at structuring tasks and interacting with students in ways that promote SRL. The observations described here are from their classrooms.

During each school year, the group met approximately one afternoon each month for 2–3 hours. Five activities provided structure to those meetings. Each meeting began with a *free write* session in which we wrote for 10 minutes about "what was on our minds" (e.g., what we'd been thinking about or trying to implement since our last meeting). Free write was followed by *air time* in which we each had 2 minutes to speak about our writing, or about something else that occurred to us as others talked. The 2 minutes provided a context in which members could air their views uninterrupted; other group members could ask for clarification but not elaboration, and could not offer evaluations or unsolicited advice. Next, we engaged in a *focus group* discussion. Topics typically arose out of issues raised at previous meetings (e.g., How can we ensure our assessments are trustworthy? To whom are we accountable? And what do they want to know?). During these focused discussions, we examined our beliefs and understandings about fostering young children's literacy, and how our beliefs and understandings get manifested in our practices. Also, we examined what current research has to say about effective teaching practices. Finally, we planned changes to our current practices during *work time* and, during the *reporting out* activity, made commitments to experiment with new teaching–learning strategies in our classrooms between our research meetings. At subsequent meetings, we had opportunities to describe and evaluate how our experiments fared during air time, and to seek advice from other community members during focus group and work time.

Time and emphasis given to each of these activities changed over the course of our work with teachers. In our first few meetings, little time was devoted to work time because teachers were unclear about the specific tasks and assessments they wanted to develop. They were more interested in discussing general issues and questions about early literacy development and the types of goals and activities they should set to foster independent, academically effective forms of reading and writing. At that time, the bulk of each session was devoted to the focus group activity. Later, however, as teachers became more confident and goal-directed, focus group discussions were brief or nonexistent. Teachers wanted to spend as much time as possible on their individual projects and interacting with one another in pairs or small groups about issues that related to their particular grade level or line of inquiry. This was particularly true in the 1998–1999 school year.

Observing in Classrooms

Between group meetings, the researchers visited classrooms and observed the teachers' implementations of innovations they had designed to help their students become more mindful and independent about their reading and writing. For example, in two Grade 1 and 2 classrooms, we observed teachers who initiated "sharing circle." At the end of each reading and writing period, students in these classrooms gathered in a circle with their teacher and responded to two questions, "What did you learn about yourself as a reader/writer today? What did you learn that you can do again and again?" Over time, the class generated a list of strategies they found helpful for writing (e.g., read your work over; if it doesn't make sense, erase it ... try again; use powerful words; make a plan). In a Grade 3 classroom, we observed as a teacher helped her students to acquire a repertoire of self-help strategies for identifying and coping with reading difficulties (e.g., make predictions, sound out a word, read to the end of the sentence, choose another book—"Maybe the book is too hard").

To document the efficacy of our teacher development and in-class activities, we collected teachers' free writes, videotaped air time and focus group discussions, collected samples of the tasks and assessments the teachers developed. We observed in classrooms, interviewed students, asked teachers to rate their students' motivation and achievement, and collected samples of students' work. The bulk of the evidence gathered from our teacher-development activities is presented in Perry, Walton, and Calder (1999) and Perry, Calder, and Mercer (1999). The student measures are described in detail in Perry and VandeKamp (2000) and Perry, VandeKamp, and Hoption (1999). Here our emphasis is on how classroom observations can illuminate ways that teachers foster children's metacognition, intrinsic motivation, and strategic action during reading and writing activities. Specifically, we describe how fine-grained analyses of running records can illustrate what teachers do and say to support young children's thinking and talking about the processes involved in reading and writing, and their acting out of those processes. Excerpts from air time and focus group discussions will be presented to elaborate the context for activities observed in the running records, and student outcomes will be presented as evidence of the efficacy of teachers' speech and actions. However, these data are ancillary to our main focus on the running records and, therefore, our methods of collecting them are not described in detail here.

THE RUNNING RECORDS

The Protocol

Our observation instrument (adapted from Perry, 1998) has three sections. The first provides space to record (a) whose classroom is being observed, in what school, and at what grade level, (b) who is observing, (c) the date of the observation, and (d) the nature and duration of the activity in which teachers and students are engaged during that observation (e.g., selecting a topic to research, writing an alternate ending for *The Three Little Pigs*). The second section provides space to keep a running record of "what was going on," including verbatim samples of teachers' and students' speech. The third section lists categories, derived from previous investigations, that distinguish high- and low-SRL environments, including (a) types of tasks (open or closed), (b) types of choice, (c) opportunities to control challenge, (d) opportunities for self-evaluation, (e) support from the teacher (instrumental vs. procedural), (f) support from peers, and (g) evaluation practices (mastery- or performance-oriented). This list of categories provides a conceptual framework for observing in classrooms and then coding those observations. However, observers are encouraged to refine and expand these categories through their observations. Therefore, our "schema" reflects a mix of analytic and emergent categories (Strauss, 1987).

During each observation, we position ourselves so that we can clearly see and hear the teacher and students without being intrusive. We record events and actions, including a list of times related to events and actions, and, as much as possible, verbatim speech in teacher–student and student–student interactions.

After each observation, we read and annotate our running records, adding details regarding events and actions that we did not have time to record during the observation and filling in gaps in teachers' speech with paraphrases of what they said. (Paraphrases are marked with square brackets.) Once we are satisfied that the running record is as detailed and accurate as our memories will allow, we re-read it, noting incidents and examples reflected in our original list of analytic categories in the third section of the observation instrument, as well as events and actions that suggest refinements or additions to those categories (i.e., emerging categories).

Coding

Our analyses of the running records focus on what teachers say and do to promote SRL and on evidence that students are responding. First, drawing on the list of categories in the third section of our running record, we identify instances of teachers' speech and actions during each observation that are believed to promote SRL (e.g., giving choices, engaging students in various forms of self-evaluation). Next, we assign each running record a rating of 0 or 1 for each of the overarching categories (e.g., choice, challenge, self-evaluation) to indicate the presence or absence of that quality in the activity. These ratings are entered in a summary table for each class to generate a profile of the consistency with which reading and writing activities in that classroom are high-SRL across multiple observations. Table 1 shows the proportion of times a category was noted across observations in the five classrooms in which we observed in the 1998–99 school year. Finally, we return to each instance of teacher speech and action and consider what aspect of self-regulation it promotes and how. These more detailed analyses are the focus here.

The Cases

We have selected two representative running records from two of the five classrooms in which we observed during the 1998–99 school year. One of the running records describes PM's kindergarten and Grade 1 class. The 17 students in

TABLE 1
Summary of Ratings for Reading and Writing Activities in the Five Classrooms

Variable	*PM*	*DH*	*MH*	*TS*	*BG*
Open tasks and activities	100% (7/7)	100% (9/9)	100% (8/8)	100% (7/7)	100% (5/5)
Choice					
What	100% (7/7)	56% (5/9)	100% (8/8)	100% (7/7)	100% (5/5)
Who	43% (3/7)	11% (1/9)	50% (4/8)	14% (1/7)	40% (2/5)
Where	29% (2/7)	0% (0/9)	50% (4/8)	0% (0/7)	40% (2/5)
When	43% (2/7)	0% (0/9)	13% (4/8)	0% (0/7)	40% (2/5)
Challenge	71% (5/7)	67% (6/9)	100% (8/8)	100% (7/7)	80% (4/5)
Self and other evaluation	86% (6/7)	89% (8/9)	100% (8/8)	100% (7/7)	100% (5/5)
Teacher evaluation	100% (7/7)	78% (7/9)	100% (8/8)	100% (7/7)	100% (5/5)
Teacher support	100% (7/7)	100% (9/9)	100% (8/8)	100% (7/7)	100% (5/5)
Peer support	86% (6/7)	78% (7/9)	100% (8/8)	71% (5/7)	100% (5/5)

Note. Cell values indicate the proportion of self-regulated learning ratings (ratings of 1) each category received across observations. Numbers in parentheses indicate raw scores (ratio of times observed to total observations). Reprinted from the *International Journal of Educational Research, 33,* Perry, VandeKamp, Mercer, & Nordby, "Creating Classroom Context That Support Young Children's Development of Self-Regulated Learning," 821–843, 2000, with permission from Elsevier Science.

PM's class come from a mix of low-middle, middle, and high-middle income families, and are ethnically and linguistically homogeneous (only 8% of the school's population speak English as a second language). The second running record describes MH's Grade 1 and 2 class. Students in this class ($N = 24$) come from families with low to middle incomes (mainly working class), and reflect a greater degree of diversity (more than 30% of the school's population speaks a language other than English at home).

Wharton-McDonald, Pressley, Rankin, Mistretta, Yokoi, and Ettenberger (1997) claim that one of the most striking features of the outstanding primary classrooms in which they observed was the "sheer density of the literacy instruction. … Highly effective teachers were able to integrate multiple goals into single lessons and could weave together strands from different lessons to form coherent, meaningful patterns of instruction" (p. 520). This was certainly the case for the two teachers we profile in this manuscript. The running record from PM's class describes the continuation of reading and writing activities based on *The Three Little Pigs*. The lesson (April 13, 1999) begins with a re-reading of the story in which PM prompts students' use of tracking and decoding strategies and practices predicting and connection strategies to support comprehension and to prepare for the writing activity that followed. The writing activity was a continuation of a sequencing task—children had created a "story strip" for *The Three Little Pigs* in a previous lesson. Today's goal was to have children rewrite the story's ending (the pigs boil the wolf in a big pot) after giving consideration to their recent discussions about how consequences should fit the crime (e.g., "If someone does something mean to you, should you be mean back?" PM). In this instructional sequence, PM addressed multiple goals for reading, writing, and social and moral reasoning. Also reflected in this sequence is PM's overarching goal of helping beginning readers and writers to attend to the communicative and meaningful aspects of reading and writing, as well as the mechanical aspects, which, understandably, capture much of their attention at this stage in their literacy development (Perry, 1998).

The example we have selected from MH's class describes the first of many reading and writing periods spent on researching a mammal. One of MH's goals for this lesson (November 3, 1999) was to determine what her students knew about mammals and to provide them with some background information. Toward this end, she introduced and read a book on mammals. A second goal was to have students distinguish between factual and fictional writing. Her third goal differed for Grade 1 and 2 students; she wanted her Grade 1 students to attempt some factual writing and her Grade 2 students to choose a mammal as a topic for a research project. In this lesson, we observed MH very successfully juggle multiple and discrepant goals for two groups of students. MH's overarching teaching goal for the 1998 through 1999 school year was to examine how what she said to students and how the discourse of the classroom influenced students' awareness of and ability to perform reading and writing processes. This running record is an excellent example of how MH promoted students' metacognition and strategic action in the context of meaningful literacy activities.

WHAT DID TEACHERS DO AND SAY TO PROMOTE SRL?

We use five overarching categories from our observation protocol to organize what PM and MH did to support SRL: They gave students choices, opportunities to control challenge, opportunities to evaluate their own and others' learning, instrumental support, and feedback and evaluation that was nonthreatening and mastery-oriented. These categories are not mutually exclusive (e.g., often, choices offered opportunities to control challenge). Moreover, much of what these teachers did to promote SRL is captured in our running records by our verbatim recording of what they said. Therefore, we present evidence for these two variables concurrently.

Offered Choices

In PM's class, students had choices about how the story of *The Three Little Pigs* would be read ("Should we have shared reading or …?") and how to follow along as the story was read (e.g., to track or not to track). Both these choices offered students opportunities to "set" the level of challenge and to make a decision based on a quick evaluation of their skills as readers:

> If you're someone who needs to follow with your finger. … If you don't need to do that … you can keep up without. … We're starting to have some choices about that. (PM)

Further into the "shared" story reading, one student had difficulty deciphering a word. PM asked all students, "[Student's name] came to a clunk.[1] What could [student's name] do?" Here students had an opportunity to choose from their repertoire of decoding strategies one they thought could solve this reading problem. The class tried each strategy suggested until they successfully decoded the difficult word. In this way, students also evaluated the efficacy of each strategy suggested until they found one that worked.

During the discussion of alternate story endings for *The Three Little Pigs*, PM's students had several opportunities to share their ideas with a peer of their choice. Also, they were encouraged to choose a side in discussing the issue of whether the pigs were acting appropriately in avenging the wolf. Ultimately, each student chose an alternate ending for their rendi-

[1] In the language of PM's class, a "clunk" was a reading miscue. "Clicking along" meant reading fluently without errors.

tion of *The Three Little Pigs,* and they chose where to do their writing ("If you want to work on the floor, that's fine").

Similarly, students in MH's class made many decisions concerning what and how they would learn during the lesson described in our running record. After reading the book on mammals to the class, MH indicated to students that they could choose that book during their "shared" reading time. (In MH's class, shared reading occurred during the first half hour of each morning and involved children reading with children, with parents, or with the teacher.) Later, MH asked her Grade 1 students, "What can you write about?" and students were quick to say, "Anything." Grade 2 students spent the bulk of this lesson "choosing" a topic for their research projects, choosing materials that would help them do their research, and beginning to decide what kind of information they would gather about their topic. Students chose where in the room to work and some students chose to work with a partner.

Offered Opportunities to Control Challenge

We have already described how PM offered opportunities for her students to control challenge by giving them choices. PM also challenged or relieved students according to her goals and expectations for them. In this lesson, she challenged students by saying, "I want everyone to come up with at least one idea." However, she also made it possible for all students to meet that challenge by having them share their ideas with a friend, and later with her, and by recording students' ideas on chart paper so that they could refer to their own or other children's ideas when they wrote their story ending. "Writing" in PM's class could take the form of drawing. For kindergarten and Grade 1 students who found it difficult to provide a detailed rendering of their ideas with print, PM often suggested they begin with drawing. By drawing first, her emergent writers got their ideas down before they were forgotten. The drawings served as a plan or outline and the writing followed, thus easing the burden on working memory of keeping ideas in mind and representing those ideas with print. In this lesson, students drew their endings and PM relieved students who wouldn't complete their drawings in this writing session while at the same time challenging those who did finish to go a bit further (e.g., "You only need to draw today, but if you have a few extra minutes. ...").

Like PM, MH enabled students to control challenge by making choices. She accepted "anything" as a response to her question, "What can you write about?" However, she also challenged students to try writing something factual. First, she encouraged students by suggesting, "If you are an expert on [something ... you might write facts about that]." Then, when students said they could write about anything, she promoted factual writing further by saying, "Can you choose to write something factual?" Some students did choose this less familiar genre for their writing that day, and MH continued to encourage their efforts by saying, "You're doing some nonfiction writing. ... You're an expert on dogs. ... You know a lot about dogs." Also, like PM, MH accepted drawing as writing and other forms of emergent writing. This enabled students to modify task demands to match their level of expertise in writing. The Grade 1 students' writing books were unlined. However, MH was quick to recognize when a student was ready to move to the next level of literacy and to encourage that movement. In checking one child's "writing," she commented, "I notice you are more interested in writing than pictures. I think we should put some lines [on your page]." This student nodded agreeably and appeared enthusiastic. Finally, as was the case in our sample lesson from PM's class, the content and discourse in MH's lesson were complex (e.g., What's the difference between factual and fictional text? What's an index? How do you use it? Are you an expert at anything?), and would challenge students in higher grades than MH's students. However, like PM, MH provided young students with the support they needed to be successful in challenging activities. She created an optimally challenging but nonthreatening environment for students to develop and exercise attributes associated with SRL.

Offered Opportunities for Students to Evaluate Self and Others

Opportunities for students to evaluate themselves and others were less a target of instruction in this lesson than in other lessons we observed in PM's class. One of our running records describes how PM's students selected samples of their work to share with their parents during student-led conferences (March 2, 1999). To guide students choices, PM asked, "What were we doing that we're proud of? What can you share with your parents? What can we do that we couldn't do before?" In this lesson, however, there were opportunities for students to review and reflect on themselves as learners (e.g., "If you are someone who needs to follow with your finger. ..."), and to provide feedback to others (e.g., "What could [student's name do]?"). In addition, PM offered opportunities for students to evaluate the feelings and actions of characters in the text they were studying. For example, she asked students to take the perspective of the mother pig ("We never talked about the mother. How do you think she felt?"), and she asked students to evaluate the actions of the pigs ("Should the pigs have put the wolf in the hot pot?") in relation to a discussion about what is right or wrong for them to do ("Remember, we talked about if someone does something mean to you. Should you be mean back?"). Finally, PM almost always followed a request for students' suggestions or opinions with a request for an explanation about why that would be an appropriate thing to do ("Let's talk about why"). In this way, students were encouraged to be mindful about whether and why a particular strategy worked, whether an answer was correct, or why they thought or felt a particular way.

MH also embedded opportunities for students to monitor and evaluate their learning in class discussions about reading and writing. When she introduced the book about mammals to her students, she prompted them to be thinking about how "this book is different from the other books I've been reading. I'm not going to tell you how it's different." Then MH asked students to keep their predictions in their heads and to be "thinking about whether they match" the information she read from the text. When she assigned the Grade 1 students their writing task, she invited them to think about whether they "are an expert on [something]." Later, when she met with students individually to go over their writing, she asked each one to judge whether their writing was fiction or nonfiction. Similarly, when she assigned Grade 2 students the task of choosing a research topic, she asked that they consider three questions: "Am I interested [in this topic]? Can I find books [about this topic]? Can I read the books by myself, with a friend, with an adult?" Consideration of these questions required that students evaluate characteristics of themselves as learners, the demands of the task they were undertaking, and the strategies available to them if they experienced some difficulty. Finally, at the end of the lesson, MH asked students, "What did you learn about yourself as a writer today?" Students' responses (paraphrased by MH) included "You need to have some reading strategies for nonfiction reading," "You need to get started right away," and "You need to stay focused." For each of the strategies students generated, MH followed up with the question, "Can you do that again?" These were familiar questions for MH's students. She asked them at the end of every reading and writing period.

Provided Instrumental Support Through Self and Peers

In Wharton-McDonald et al.'s (1997) study, highly effective primary teachers

> Used a great deal of scaffolded instruction ... and enabled students to progress with just the right amount and level of assistance. They encouraged students to be self-regulated learners, so that students could continue to learn and progress on their own. (p. 520)

Often, PM and MH were agents of their students' self-regulation, providing just enough support to ensure students' application of independent, academically effective forms of learning. In this way, their support was instrumental as opposed to being merely procedural.

At the beginning of the reading activity described in our running record from PM's class, PM asked students where they might look in their anthologies if they couldn't remember the page on which *The Three Little Pigs* begins: "If we forget what page ... and we want to find out real quick, where can we look ... what's that page called?" Rather than directing students to turn to the table of contents to find the page where the story starts, or just directing them to the correct page, PM asked a question that enabled students to enact an effective strategy on their own. Similarly, instead of correcting a student's reading miscue, she asked all students to think what could be done to decipher the difficult word, prompting students to draw from their arsenal of effective decoding strategies and solve the problem independent of their teacher. In other instances, she provided students with information they might need to make an appropriate choice or modify an activity to an appropriate level of challenge: "If you're someone who needs to follow along with your finger. ... If ... you can keep up without. ..." Then she allowed students to make the choice but monitored the efficacy of their decision. In this example, one child chose not to track the text during the shared reading activity and lost his place. When PM asked, "Everybody read this sentence," she identified this student, showed him the correct place and prompted him to begin tracking, all without interrupting the reading activity. Through this subtle intervention, PM intended to communicate, "What you're doing is not working. Tracking should help."

PM often created opportunities for students to provide instrumental support to one another. In this lesson, students helped one another to solve decoding and comprehension problems, and they shared ideas during their prewriting discussion. PM fostered a community of learners where listening to, even appropriating, other students' ideas was valued. In the discussion about whether the pigs had acted appropriately in punishing the wolf, one student indicated that she had changed her mind. PM responded, "That's OK," and followed up by asking, "What changed your mind? ... Was it listening to other people's opinions?" Similarly, MH's students had many opportunities to learn from one another because there was so much discussion about learning in their classroom. In our sample running record, MH asked her students to share their ideas about "the smartest animal in the world" and how the book she read them that morning differed from books she had read to them in the past. She invited Grade 2 students to work with one another to consider the three questions she posed regarding their choice of a research topic. Finally, at the end of the lesson, students shared what they had learned about themselves as writers that day and what they had learned that they could use in the future. "Sharing circle" was a familiar participation structure in MH's class. It had occurred at the end of most reading and writing periods since September. Some days, MH recorded students ideas on chart paper to build inventories of how students were becoming "good readers and writers," and to document the range of strategies available to them for handling all varieties of reading and writing problems.

Like PM, MH was more likely to ask a question that would help students to solve a problem or generate an understanding than to correct an error or supply information directly, particularly if the information to be acquired involved high levels of thinking or metacognition. Her strategy was to provide the cue that would initiate students' thought experiments (e.g., "This is different than other books I've been reading. I'm not going to tell you how it's different. … Be thinking. …"). MH often engaged in self-talk to model her thought processes for students (e.g., "Sometimes the hardest thing [is to choose a topic]"), or pointed to students' actions or work samples that exemplified something she wanted students to be aware of or learn (e.g., "You're doing some nonfiction writing," "I learned something about you today," "You learned that you need to have some reading strategies [for nonfiction reading]"). Finally, MH often recapped students' responses to her questions with elaboration or with a follow-up question that challenged students to think more deeply about their response. Typically, her prompts began with open-ended queries ("Tell me more about that? What was it that you did today?") and became increasingly specific depending on the amount of support students required to respond correctly (e.g., "Did you get started right away? Did you stay focused?").

These examples demonstrate that, with the kind of instrumental support PM and MH provide, young children are able to function at high levels, thinking metacognitively and acting strategically. Also they demonstrate that instrumental support requires highly skilled teachers who know what they want to accomplish and "how to make it happen" (Wharton-McDonald et al., 1997, p. 520). Both PM and MH had a clear sense of purpose and high expectations concerning what their young students could know and do. They also thought very carefully about what they, as teachers, would need to do to help their students meet their goals. For example, during the group meeting that preceded our observation of *The Three Little Pigs* activities, PM described a workshop she had been to that was "really geared toward Grade 5 and 6 students" (PM, April 7, 1999). However, PM said, "The ideas were very attractive to me, so I took some of what [the presenter] said and did it on a very primary level, and very oral. It was a lot of oral discussion as opposed to written." After this explanation, one of the other teachers in our group commented, "You know, that's great … because … there was a kindergarten teacher sitting next to me [at the same workshop] that said, 'This is just too old for [my students].' … It was too bad" (TS, April 7, 1999).

Evaluation was Nonthreatening and Mastery Oriented

A hallmark of high SRL environments is that they challenge students without threatening their self-efficacy. In these environments, assessment and evaluation are ongoing, embedded in daily activities, focused on personal progress, and promote a view that errors are opportunities to learn (Paris, Lawton, & Turner, 1992; Pintrich, Marx, & Boyle, 1993; Rohrkemper & Corno, 1988.) Such nonthreatening evaluation practices are represented in our running record of PM's class, even though she was not grading students or providing them with detailed feedback on a particular assignment. When PM involved the entire class in solving one student's decoding problem, she was using that student's error as an opportunity for all students to learn the "problem" word and practice their decoding strategies. Later, when another student gave an incorrect answer to a comprehension question, PM asked the group if they agreed and then, together, they found the correct answer. Singling students out in this way could be upsetting for the child who made the mistake. However, in PM's class, these discussions were a natural part of each instructional event. The tone was helpful, not critical. The message was that "everyone makes mistakes, that's OK, everyone needs help sometimes, and everyone learns by helping."

PM made her students accountable for thinking and learning, but in a nonthreatening way. For example, by randomly selecting student readers during the shared reading activity, PM ensured most students were actively following along and ready to participate. When a student was caught not following, PM asked another student to carry on reading while she went to the student who was off task, pointed to the place where he should be, and prompted him to track the text with his finger so that she could be sure he was following along. Similarly, when a student offered an ending to *The Three Little Pigs* that was the same or similar to the original ending, PM said, "I was hoping we'd change the ending. I'll give you another minute." Rather than putting the student on the spot by having to generate a different ending immediately, she challenged the student to think of a new idea and indicated she would check it in "another minute." In these interactions, PM communicated to students that she expected high levels of achievement from them. However, she also communicated that she would help them to be successful. Notice that no child was left with an error uncorrected. The decoding error, the comprehension mistake, and unoriginal story endings were all corrected before the lesson ended and students left the group to work independently. In fact, PM asked all students to describe their writing ideas to her before leaving the group to work independently, and asked one student to stay behind to discuss his idea ("[Student's name] stay here a minute. I'm not sure about that one"). By creating a nonthreatening environment and ensuring each student's success, PM promoted a mastery orientation to learning; students were encouraged to persist in challenging circumstances, and to focus on learning and personal progress.

MH also created a challenging but nonthreatening evaluation context for her students. In addition to turning students' errors or omissions into opportunities to learn (e.g., "One thing I'd like you to do tomorrow …"), she often told students about mistakes she made, things she forgot to do, or things she was learning (e.g., "I learned something about you today"). Like PM, MH held students accountable for their learning but made sure they had the knowledge and support they needed to be successful in her teaching–learning environment. In our example, she checked Grade 1 students' understanding of their writing task before asking them to work independently, and informed them that she would want to "conference" with them when they were done. Later, she met with students individually to read their writing and offered praise and corrective feedback ("I like … One thing I'd like you to do tomorrow …"). Similarly, as Grade 2 students considered books as potential resources for their research project, MH reminded them to check whether they could read the books ("If you haven't checked that, do it now"), and she informed them that she would be asking them to "tell me something you've discovered about your animal. You're going to report back to me in five minutes." Finally, as was the case in PM's class, students were never put on the spot in a punitive way. If, in checking a students' understanding, MH discovered a child was having difficulty, she either gave the student more time (as she did during sharing circle when she "came back" to students who weren't ready), or worked with the student to solve his or her learning problems (as she did during conferences with Grade 1 students about their writing).

STUDENT OUTCOMES

Although our primary focus has been on what teachers do and say to promote SRL, it seems appropriate to end with a summary of how students benefit when teachers design tasks and interact with them in the ways PM and MH did. In Perry's original study (1998), students in high-SRL classrooms adopted skills and attitudes that are characteristic of self-regulated learners, whereas children in low-SRL classrooms adopted attitudes and actions that have been associated with defensive and self-handicapping approaches to learning (Covington, 1992). For example, Perry observed Grade 2 and 3 students in high-SRL classrooms engaging in complex writing activities, such as researching and writing about a topic, and managing all aspects of the writing process independently, flexibly, and recursively. Students in these classrooms monitored and evaluated their writing progress in productive ways and sought instrumental support from their peers and teachers when they experienced difficulties. Moreover, in interviews, these students communicated attitudes and approaches to learning that focused on learning and personal progress. Even the low-achieving students in these classrooms had high efficacy for learning and did not shy away from challenging tasks. In contrast, students in low-SRL classrooms were more focused on their teachers' evaluations of their work (e.g., how many they got right on a particular assignment, and whether or not they got stickers). In these classes, low-achieving students especially, avoided challenging tasks and, in interviews, communicated perceptions of low ability and low efficacy for learning. Finally, Perry observed students in these classes passing over, or even rejecting, opportunities to regulate some aspect of their learning and choosing academically ineffective strategies such as procrastinating and hiding their work.

Since that original study, we have observed changes in student attitudes and actions that link to our work with teachers. For example, at the end of our first year of collaborating with teachers (Spring 1998), 64% of the students we interviewed indicated that errors made them feel unhappy, and 47% indicated that they believed errors made their teacher unhappy. At the end of our second year, the year from which our sample running records were drawn, only 37% of the students we interviewed reported negative affect as a response to errors, and only 22% indicated their teacher experienced negative affect when she observed children making mistakes. In addition, the proportion of students indicating a preference for easy tasks decreased from 50% to 26% from year one to year two. These findings are in line with our goal of promoting views that errors are opportunities to learn and challenging tasks are worthwhile and fun. Finally, students in both years provided us with a list of strategies they use, or recommend others use, when faced with challenging reading or writing tasks. A summary of these strategies is presented in Table 2. Although the strategies they report are much less sophisticated than those reported by more mature learners, they do list both general executive and domain specific tactics that reflect the broader categories of strategies that self-regulated learners use (e.g., modifying tasks to control challenge, applying specific strategies to cope with the meaningful or mechanical aspects of reading and writing).

At one of our group meetings, PM described what her students learned by engaging in activities like the one described in our example:

> I thought, very naturally, a debate came out of it. … They realized that some questions are really difficult to answer. … It isn't so black and white. So it was a really excellent discussion. … The book … was quite difficult for them to read. … We read it together. … I read some and they read some. And they handled it and it was really neat to see them doing that. (PM, July 4, 1999)

PM also noticed the impact this activity had on her students' motivation:

> I found that, particularly during the discussion, there wasn't anybody that wasn't engaged, which is not always the case with my group. … I looked around and everybody was really into what we were doing. And we went for 40 minutes, which is, for them … a long time to be doing one thing. (PM, July 4, 1999)

At the same meeting, MH described how she and her students "talk so much more about reading now and we do so much more reading." Also, MH described how the students were enacting the "talk" she was modeling in her classroom.

> One morning, when MH was reading with a child, "he came to the word puffin and he figured it out. … I said, 'Well how did you know that?' [He said], 'I just knew that word.' I said, 'Oh, OK,' and then he said, 'I like that word puffin.' … I'm always talking about … like the word 'lurking.' And then he says, 'Say that word.' I said, 'Puffin.' [He said], 'Doesn't it

TABLE 2
Strategies Students Recommended or Reported Using to Cope With Reading and Writing Difficulties

Strategy	*Examples*
Help seeking (78%)	Ask for help from teacher or peer Get ideas from other people Get someone who knows how to write Get some help on spelling Ask your mom to check it over Ask an older student (in the case of split classes)
Modifying tasks to control challenge (33%)	Write shorter stories Do little words Write journals instead—What you did on the weekend Write easier stories Make a story that you know how to spell
Persisting or increasing effort (30%)	Practice more at home and school Write it again Pay attention to the teacher Try very, very hard I do my best
Applying strategies to cope with meaningful aspects of reading and writing (37%)	Read stories (to get ideas for writing) Think up ideas and put them together Sit and think about what you can write about Read your work over (may mean proofreading for spelling errors)
Applying strategies to cope with mechanical aspects of reading and writing (67%)	Look in a book to find the correct spelling Look at spelling cards Clap words out, write it down, check it Clap out words, say it slowly, check for patterns Sound out words Look in your word book or around the classroom Skip it, hum it
Other (11%)	I sometimes get a bit mad I just do it I write quickly
Don't know or no strategy offered (19%)	

Note. Proportions in parentheses indicate the proportions of students (percentage of 27) recommending or reporting the use of particular strategies. Reprinted from the *International Journal of Educational Research, 33,* Perry, VandeKamp, Mercer, & Nordby, "Creating Classroom Context That Support Young Children's Development of Self-Regulated Learning," 821–843, 2000, with permission from Elsevier Science.

> sound neat?' ... It was so good because all that stuff that you're talking about ... some of them are getting it. ..." (MH, July 4, 1999)

We might add that MH's students are not only getting it (witness the level of metalinguistic awareness evidenced in the above conversation), some of them are ready to teach it.

SUMMARY AND CONCLUSIONS

We have summarized our program of research which seeks to (a) identify features of classroom literacy tasks, authority structures, and evaluation practices that support young children's development of and engagement in SRL, and (b) work with teachers to design tasks and interact with students in ways that foster this approach to learning early in children's school careers. Particularly, we have highlighted the utility of conducting in-depth observations in classrooms for identifying what teachers say and do to support young children's thinking and talking about themselves as readers and writers, and the processes involved in reading and writing. Our observations, in the form of running records, confirmed that young children can and do engage in SRL in classrooms where they have opportunities to engage in complex open-ended activities, make choices that have an impact on their learning, control challenge, and evaluate themselves and others. In addition, our observations revealed the ways in which teachers provide instrumental support to students (e.g., through questioning, clarifying, correcting, elaborating, modeling) and create opportunities for students to support one another (e.g., through collaborating, sharing ideas, and brainstorming problem-solving strategies). Last but not least, we observed how teachers created nonthreatening and intrinsically motivating learning contexts by embedding assessment and evaluation in the ongoing activities of their classrooms, making students accountable without being punitive, and encouraging students to focus on personal progress and view errors as opportunities to learn. In these contexts, students demonstrated attitudes and actions that are aligned with independent, academically effective learners: metacognition, intrinsic motivation, and strategic action (Zimmerman, 1990).

Our research supports claims that observations have three important strengths as measures of SRL (Winne & Perry, 2000). First, they reflect what learners actually do versus what they say they do. Second, they illuminate links between features of the teaching–learning context (e.g., what teachers do and say) and students' engagement in SRL. These two contributions reflect an important development in research about SRL. Increasingly, researchers are looking for ways to provide more fine-grained descriptions of SRL as an event (i.e., as it unfolds in real contexts and real time). Our running records offer the potential to mark an opportunity for students to engage in SRL (e.g., teacher offers choice and opportunity to control challenge through that choice), and then to observe whether, in fact, they do (What choice does the student make? How might the choice create further opportunities for SRL to occur?). The third benefit, which we have realized in our work, is that observations are particularly helpful for studying young children's engagement in SRL. Not only do they ameliorate the difficulties associated with assessing young children's SRL (e.g., positive response bias and limited language for describing cognitive processes), they illuminate the nature and degree of support young children require to be self-regulating, and offer insights into teaching practices that promote (or curtail) young children's SRL.

In addition to recognizing the strengths of observational methods, we believe it is important to address several limitations. First, it is important to recognize that there are some aspects of SRL that are impossible to observe (metacognitive processes such as planning and monitoring are often covert). Also, it is important for researchers to recognize that what is observed often reflects a view about what is important to observe. Our observations were framed by our interest in SRL, our understandings about what supports SRL, and our knowledge of what the teachers participating in our study were trying to accomplish with their students. Although we made every effort to be open to emergent categories, we learned that it was impossible to capture everything teachers said and did, and every student's response, in a single running record. We may have missed something important. For these reasons, we recommend the use of multiple methods to triangulate findings from observations. In our research, we use semistructured interviews to check and compliment our classroom observations. In addition, we believe it is important not to lose sight of the forest for the trees. We have found it most enlightening to continually move back and forth between our detailed descriptions of single events and our summaries of what occurs across multiple classrooms or in individual classrooms over time.

ACKNOWLEDGMENT

The research described in this article was supported by the Social Sciences and Humanities Research Council of Canada (No. 410–97–1366).

REFERENCES

Borko, H., & Putnam, R. (1998). Professional development and reform-based teaching: Introduction to theme issue. *Teaching and Teacher Education, 14,* 1–3.

Cain, K. M., & Dweck, C. S. (1995). The relation between motivational patterns and achievement cognitions through the elementary school years. *Merrill-Palmer Quarterly, 41,* 25–52.

Covington, M. V. (1992). *Making the grade: A self-worth perspective on motivation and school reform.* New York: Cambridge University Press.

Lave, J., & Wenger, E. (1991). *Situated learning: Legitimate peripheral participation.* New York: Cambridge University Press.

Palincsar, A. S., Magnusson, S. J., Morano, N., Ford, D., & Brown, N. (1998). Designing a community of practice: Principles and practices of the GIsML community. *Teaching and Teacher Education, 14,* 5–19.

Paris, S. G., Lawton, T. A., & Turner, J. C. (1992). Reforming achievement testing to promote students' learning. In C. Collins & J. N. Mangieri (Eds.), *Teaching thinking* (pp. 223–241). Hillsdale, NJ: Lawrence Erlbaum Associates, Inc.

Paris, S. G., & Newman, R. S. (1990). Developmental aspects of self-regulated learning. *Educational Psychologist, 25,* 87–102.

Perry, N. E. (1998). Young children's self-regulated learning and contexts that support it. *Journal of Educational Psychology, 90,* 715–729.

Perry, N. E., Calder, K., & Mercer, L. (1999, April). *What do teachers learn in a community of practice? How do they change?* Paper presented at the annual meeting of the American Educational Research Association, Montreal, Canada.

Perry, N. E., & VandeKamp, K. O. (2000). Creating classroom contexts that support young children's development of self-regulated learning. *International Journal of Educational Research, 33,* 821–843.

Perry, N. E., VandeKamp, K. O., & Hoption, C. (1999, June). Young children's motivation for writing and factors associated with it. In N. E. Perry (Chair), *Critical issues in the study and promotion of self-regulated learning.* Symposium conducted at the meeting of the Canadian Society for Studies in Education, Sherbrooke, Canada.

Perry, N. E., Walton, C., & Calder, K. (1999). Teachers developing assessments of early literacy: A community of practice project. *Teacher Education and Special Education, 22,* 218–233.

Pintrich, P. R., Marx, R. W., & Boyle, R. A. (1993). Beyond cold conceptual change: The role of motivational beliefs and classroom contextual factors in the process of conceptual change. *Review of Educational Research, 63,* 167–199.

Pressley, M., Forrest-Pressley, D. L., Elliott-Faust, D., & Miller, G. (1985). Children's use of cognitive strategies, how to teach strategies, and what to do if they can't be taught. In M. Pressley and C. J. Brainerd (Eds.), *Cognitive learning and memory in children* (pp. 1–47). New York: Springer-Verlag.

Rohrkemper, M. & Corno, L. (1988). Success and failure on classroom tasks: Adaptive learning and classroom teaching. *Elementary School Journal, 88,* 297–312.

Strauss, A. L. (1987). *Qualitative Analysis for Social Scientists.* New York: Cambridge University Press.

Wharton-McDonald, R., Pressley, M., Rankin, J., Mistretta, J., Yokoi, L., & Ettenberger, S. (1997). Effective primary-grades literacy instruction = Balanced literacy instruction. *The Reading Teacher, 50,* 518–521.

Winne, P. H. (1995). Inherent details in self-regulated learning. *Educational Psychologist, 30,* 173–187.

Winne, P. H., & Perry, N. E. (2000). Measuring self-regulated learning. In P. Pintrich, M. Boekaerts, & M. Zeidner (Eds.), *Handbook of self-regulation.* Orlando, FL: Academic.

Zimmerman, B. J. (1990). Self-regulated learning and academic achievement: An overview. *Educational Psychologist, 25,* 3–17.

EDUCATIONAL PSYCHOLOGIST, 37(1), 17–25

Using Instructional Discourse Analysis to Study the Scaffolding of Student Self-Regulation

Debra K. Meyer
Department of Education
Elmhurst College

Julianne C. Turner
Department of Psychology
University of Notre Dame

This article describes how scaffolded instruction during whole-class mathematics lessons can provide the knowledge, skills, and supportive context for developing students' self-regulatory processes. In examining classroom interactions through discourse analysis, these qualitative methods reflect a theoretical change from viewing self-regulation as an individual process to that of a social process. This article illustrates how studying instructional scaffolding through the analyses of instructional discourse helps further the understanding of how self-regulated learning develops and is realized in mathematics classrooms. Qualitative methods, such as discourse analyses, and their underlying theoretical frameworks have great potential to help "unlock" theories of learning, motivation, and self-regulation through exploring the reciprocity of teaching and learning in classrooms.

To better understand self-regulation, studying the contexts in which self-regulatory processes emerge is critical. Although the importance of the classroom context in motivation has been well-established (e.g., Anderman & Anderman, 2000; Urdan, 1999), the role of context has been peripheral in the study of self-regulated learning. Difficulties in integrating "context" may be due to the arduous tasks of defining and investigating it. For example, Weiner (1996) argued that traditionally motivation research has produced limited findings due to the failure to integrate social context. He concluded that historically researchers decontextualized constructs to better suit them for experimental studies, which maintained a research agenda of presenting constructs as distinct and unrelated. Therefore, to study self-regulated learning in context requires complexity in both theory and methods.

CAPTURING CLASSROOM CONTEXT THEORETICALLY

In social-cognitive theory the relationship between the environment and the individual has been one of related, but distinct, constructs. Pintrich (2000) noted that some models of self-regulation assume that the environment is separate from the self. For example, Zimmerman's (1989) frequently quoted definition of self-regulation focuses on *individuals* as "metacognitively, motivationally, and behaviorally active participants in their own learning process" (p. 4). This perspective emphasizes how students select and choose appropriate actions and how environmental influences might help them develop these skills (Pintrich, 2000). Social-cognitive classroom research involves examining how teachers influence the development of self-regulation through modeling, social guidance, and feedback (e.g., Schunk & Zimmerman, 1996). Furthermore, much of the research on self-regulation has examined the individual differences among self-regulatory processes and minimally explored the role of classroom context in supporting their development and enactment in real classrooms.

Pintrich's (2000) definition of self-regulated learning as "an active, constructive process whereby learners set goals for their learning and then attempt to monitor, regulate, and control their cognition, motivation, and behavior, guided and constrained by their goals and the contextual features of the environment" (p. 453) illustrates how researchers have begun to articulate more complex theoretical notions of academic self-regulation. The addition of "context" to a definition of self-regulated learning is significant, but it continues to pro-

Requests for reprints should be sent to Debra K. Meyer, Department of Education, Elmhurst College, 190 Prospect Avenue, Elmhurst, IL 60126. E-mail: debram@elmhurst.edu

mote multiple interpretations of "environment" (e.g., Zimmerman, 2001). The social-cognitive perspective assumed a "triadic reciprocality" among cognitions, behaviors, and environments (Schunk & Zimmerman, 1996). However, constructivist (e.g., Paris, Byrnes, & Paris, 2001) and sociocultural (e.g., McCaslin & Hickey, 2001a, 2001b; Yowell & Smylie, 1999) perspectives on self-regulation offer different conceptualizations of "context" and "reciprocity." Such alternative theoretical perspectives about the relationship between the individual and various levels of context challenge researchers to ask different research questions and explore them in qualitatively different ways.

Sociocultural approaches assume that self-regulation is achieved through social interaction and has multiple outcomes, academic and nonacademic, which are understood within context (McCaslin & Hickey, 2001a, 2001b; Yowell & Smylie, 1999). For example, Yowell and Smylie (1999) argued that a focus on the individual inaccurately implied that regulation is only an intrapsychological process and ignores the roles of others and the social context in self-regulation. They define self-regulation as "the intentional and planful pursuit of goals in a manner that is flexible and that promotes individual growth and social change" (Yowell & Smylie, 1999, p. 471). The development and support of self-regulation occurs through reciprocal interactions among individuals and social-context elements. Such contextualized frameworks also infer reciprocity between teacher and student that evolves through *co-regulation* (McCaslin & Good, 1996; McCaslin & Hickey, 2001b). Co-regulation emphasizes the shared responsibility among teachers and students for establishing and maintaining relationships as they coordinate multiple goals through available opportunities and scaffolding supports (McCaslin & Hickey, 2001b). Thus viewing classroom learning as a negotiated process between an individual and others (e.g., Rogoff, 1990) and autonomy as a relationship, rather than an individual attribute, suggests that self-regulation may be better understood as a social process.

As researchers move toward more contextualized frameworks of self-regulation and view the relationship between individual and context as central, their research methods need to align with these theoretical perspectives. Such alternative conceptualizations are still in their infancies, both in terms of increasing our theoretical knowledge (e.g., Zimmerman & Schunk, 2001) and in employing appropriate methodologies for studying these complex social interactions.

STUDYING INSTRUCTIONAL SCAFFOLDING THROUGH CLASSROOM DISCOURSE ANALYSIS

Qualitative methods have increasingly supported motivation researchers in providing descriptions of the classroom contexts in which students report the greatest motivation to learn and teacher support (e.g., Blumenfeld & Meece, 1988; Meece, 1991; Patrick, Anderman, Ryan, Edelin, & Midgley, 2001; Stipek et al., 1998; Turner et al., in press). Important links between teachers' instructional responses and students' motivation and self-regulation also have been established (e.g., Perry & VandeKamp, 2000; Turner, 1995). Thus qualitative research has begun to enrich the literature on self-regulation through studies of teachers' instructional practices that provide the opportunities for self-regulation in real classroom contexts.

These qualitative research findings include vivid descriptions of scaffolded instruction and its potential for supporting students' development of self-regulation. Scaffolding is an instructional process in which a teacher supports students cognitively, motivationally, and emotionally in learning while helping them to further develop autonomy. The metaphor of scaffolding (Wood, Bruner, & Ross, 1976) is based on Vygotsky's (1978) concept of the "zone of proximal development" (ZPD), or the conceptual space between learners' current competencies and what they can achieve with the support of more knowledgeable others. Scaffolding is an inherently social process, one shared between experts and novices, parents and children, or teachers and students. During instructional scaffolding, the teacher supports student self-regulation, as needed, in three ways: (a) helping students build competence through increased understanding, (b) engaging students in learning while supporting their socioemotional needs, and (c) helping students build and exercise autonomy as learners. An integral component of effective scaffolding is *intersubjectivity*, or "a shared understanding between teacher and student of a problem-solving task within the ZPD," which requires "mutual trust, respect, and the communication skills necessary to bridge the distance between expert and novice" (Yowell & Smylie, 1999, p. 474).

Therefore, researching scaffolding requires methods that are situated in classrooms and can explore the complexities of teacher–student interactions. Borrowing from sociolinguistic methodologies, we use discourse analysis as a qualitative methodology for exploring classroom interactions. Sociolinguistic methods highlight the "mediational role of discourse and joint activity" (Hicks, 1996, p. 55) and explore the multiple levels of context through language, which "weaves the fabric of classroom culture" (Alvermann & Hayes, 1989, p. 305). In other words, classroom talk is our window into the social process of self-regulation.

In the following sections, we outline our discourse method for studying instructional scaffolding during mathematics lessons, including the coding and analyses of this qualitative data. Then we present excerpts from a classroom lesson to illustrate how instructional discourse patterns reveal contexts that support self-regulation.

INVESTIGATING INSTRUCTIONAL SCAFFOLDING DURING MATHEMATICS LESSONS

Two contextual features are unique to our study of instructional scaffolding. First, we examine scaffolding during whole-class interactions. Most studies of scaffolding have been conducted with parent–child dyads, or in tutoring or small-group instruction. Second, we investigate classroom interactions during mathematics lessons. Subject area is a salient contextual feature in classroom learning, which influences what counts as knowledge and how discourse is structured.

Instructional Scaffolding in Whole-Class Interactions

As Brophy (1999) noted, the contexts of classrooms differ vastly from the experimental or self-chosen contexts in which much motivation research is conducted. First and foremost, discourse is often constrained by whole-group instructional formats, such as cycles of known-answer questions followed by short student responses that are evaluated by the teacher. Such formats make participation more risky for students and offer them fewer choices about how to participate (Mehan, 1985). These constraints on discourse stem, in part, from the large teacher-to-student ratio that works against the very kinds of knowledge parents or tutors use to interact successfully with children. For example, teachers are more limited in their immediate knowledge of the students' cognitive, motivational, emotional, and social competencies that are essential for providing appropriate instruction *when* it is needed. To gain this knowledge and effectively scaffold, teachers frequently interact verbally with twenty or more students simultaneously.

In addition to discourse constraints, classroom structures complicate many of the critical aspects of individual scaffolding interactions. For example, interactions are constrained by time demands (e.g., math periods have beginning and ending times), which limit teachers' choices of instructional activities and student choices regarding engagement. Classrooms also are challenging places for promoting intrinsic motivation and self-regulation because success and failure are public and the performance demands are constant (e.g., grades, tests, reports to parents), making extrinsic goals salient (Brophy, 1999) and offering limited opportunities for student choice and autonomy. Co-regulation between a teacher and twenty-some students with varying needs and competencies is highly complex in whole-class instruction.

Instructional Scaffolding in Mathematics

Contextualized perspectives in theory and methods are essential for answering questions of how teachers socialize students into domain-specific ways of learning and the differences in domain specific "ways of knowing" (Greeno, Collins, & Resnick, 1996). Subject areas, like mathematics, have traditions and discipline-specific notions of what counts as learning and teaching, which are sometimes conflicting (e.g., "right answers" vs. "process over product"). For example, when teachers and students co-regulate learning experiences during mathematics lessons they are negotiating more than conceptual differences among types of angles in a geometry unit, they are building an understanding of what it means to think and speak mathematically or to be "good" at math. Within the elementary classroom, building mathematical understanding may be as much about learning the language, tools, and skills of math as it is about learning mathematical concepts.

The constraints on scaffolding during whole-class math instruction also restrict students' opportunities to develop or demonstrate self-regulation. However, despite these constraints, we find real differences in the instructional discourse among classrooms. In response to students who are not yet capable of performing procedures or explaining concepts on their own, teachers can use either scaffolded or nonscaffolded discourse. For example, scaffolding is often characterized by teacher modeling, "hints," cueing questions, open questions, or providing a piece of the solution. Teachers might guide students through a procedure first by elaborating on a given example: "Here is a factor tree for 100 and they break it down into 25 times 4, and then they break it down further into 5 times 5 times 2 times 2. Here they took 100 and they found factors 10 times 10. And they broke each down into 2 times 5. …" Or teachers might invite possible answers from students: "What two numbers would you come up with if I asked you to find two factors of 100?" Or, teachers might ask, "What would you do next?"

If students are unsure, scaffolding may involve breaking the problem down while providing cues, as in the following example of a teacher helping a student understand the use of exponents to write a final factoring solution with a multiplication sign:

> Teacher: Okay, so the exponent—How many fives are there, Jason?
> Jason: Two.
> Teacher: Okay, and how many twos are there?
> Jason: Two.
> Teacher: Okay, what's missing? Your numbers are right. There's an operation you need to put in there between the numbers.

To check understanding before proceeding, a teacher might scaffold by asking students to decide if they need further examples (e.g., "Okay, want me to do it again?") or by offering a new problem to check their understanding (e.g., "I'm just going to make up some numbers and see if you can factor them out").

Finally, to support student autonomy, a teacher might scaffold by asking students to articulate solution paths or rationales for their approaches (e.g., "Tell me how you know that" or "Tell me how you did that") or to self-evaluate (e.g., "Which approach do you think is the best to use?"). Because the teacher makes possible the student participation, students have multiple opportunities to self-correct or evaluate approaches and solutions. In doing so, instructional scaffolding creates opportunities to build and demonstrate competence, revealing ways to learn, monitor, and evaluate, which are simultaneously supporting opportunities to self-regulate.

In nonscaffolding sequences, teacher questions limit student involvement by repeatedly asking for right answers (e.g., "2 times 8 times 15 ... Is that right or wrong?") or by asking students to do meaningless rote calculations. Such instructional sequences may play out like in the following example of a teacher factoring the number 72 on the board:

Teacher: The easiest thing to think of, 9 times 8, that's 72 right? Can 9 be lowered down to anything else?
Student: Yes.
Teacher: To what?
Student: 3 and 3.
Teacher: 3 times 3, [is] that what people thought, right?
Student: Yes.
Teacher: 8 can be lowered down to what?
Student: 2 times 4.
Teacher: Lowest 4. No, stays the same, this 3 stays the same, 2 stays the same, but the 4 can be lowered to ...
Student: 2 and 2.
Teacher: 2 times 2. So the answer, you can either write it like this (*pointing to* $2 \times 2 \times 2 \times 3 \times 3$) or any other forms right there (e.g., $2^3 \times 3^2$).

This kind of nonscaffolded discourse, especially when it forms a high proportion of classroom instruction, is less conducive to self-regulation because it affords students fewer opportunities to participate in meaningful ways and to check their understanding. Because demonstration is less likely to be accompanied by teacher explanations, there is also less metacognitive modeling for approaching a problem strategically.

CODING INSTRUCTIONAL SCAFFOLDING

To capture the majority of instructional interactions, we use a tiered coding scheme based on the theoretical definition of instructional scaffolding. Teachers' scaffolded responses are placed into three categories:

1. Scaffolding understanding through negotiation of meaning of key concepts (e.g., types of angles) and related procedures and skills (e.g., measuring angles).
2. Scaffolding autonomy through supporting student strategy use (e.g., illustrating different approaches) and transferring responsibility to students (e.g., asking students to model).
3. Scaffolding a positive classroom climate for learning through support for students' intrinsic motivation, emotional well-being, and peer collaboration.

The last category of scaffolding has evolved from our research questions and findings and includes motivational supports as well as emotional and social supports. Motivational supports emphasize the value of learning and of making progress in constructive ways and can reflect teacher humor and enthusiasm that engage students in math (cf. Brophy's, 1999, "motivational scaffolding"). Emotional support is given through teacher attention to students' emotional needs, such as responding to student anxiety, frustration, or embarrassment, or relationship-building responses (e.g., "How are you doing with that problem now?"). Social support is provided through teacher responses that establish and support a collaborative learning environment in which students support each other and share responsibility for learning.

Coding Nonscaffolded Instruction

Nonscaffolded instruction is coded into two broad categories of *teacher-controlled* responses and *nonsupportive motivational* or *socioemotional* responses. Typical examples of how teachers "take over" the discourse in instructional interactions include asking known-answer questions, evaluating students' answers as right or wrong without conceptual elaboration, or emphasizing the teacher or textbook as primary authorities. When we first began investigating such forms of teacher control in discourse, we viewed them as negative. However, we have come to realize that some of these forms of teacher control are useful at different times within a lesson to preview, review, or summarize. In addition, these instructional responses may provide opportunities for students to demonstrate competence by providing right answers or for teachers to check student progress. We now believe that it is the pattern or balance among the types of instructional discourse categories that provide the qualitatively rich understandings of what interactions are like in different classroom contexts (Turner, Meyer, Midgley, & Patrick, in press)

Teacher nonsupportive motivational or socioemotional statements include responses that emphasize performance outcomes over learning, or highlight learning activities as uninteresting, too difficult, or confusing, which are coded as examples of nonintrinsic reasons for learning. Negative or sarcastic comments about student abilities or efforts, or positive yet superficial statements that make "students feel good" in the absence of any genuine accomplishments are coded as nonsupportive forms of emotion-related interactions. Teacher responses that accentuate social comparison or discourage collaboration are considered countersupportive to those that build a positive climate.

Coding Management and Organizational Discourse

Although we currently do not address these organizational codes because of the similar proportions of their use across classrooms, teachers' responses regarding classroom management or organization also are coded as supportive or nonsupportive. *Supportive classroom management* is evidenced when teachers ensure that transitions are made smoothly, directions are given clearly, and procedures support student engagement in learning (e.g., breaking students into groups or pairs). *Nonsupportive classroom management* would be coded when teachers interrupt or disrupt engagement through publicly noting off-task behaviors (e.g., "Nicholas, raise your hand!") or making abrupt or disconnected transitions.

Discourse Coding Procedures

These *a priori* coding categories for instructional discourse are used to code the transcripts into three broad categories: (a) understanding and autonomy, (b) motivation, emotion, and social collaboration, and (c) organization and management. Within each broad category there are two subcategories, supportive or nonsupportive, and within these subcategories are more specific types of teacher responses. For example, a positive climate response would be specifically coded as supporting motivation (e.g., "That was a great try!"), supporting emotion or interpersonal relationships (e.g., "I know the feeling, I get those days too. Sometimes we wake up in fog, right?"), or supporting social collaboration (e.g., "Make sure your partner understands how you arrived at your answer").

Each coded teacher response can range from a single word to the entire speaking turn. The categorization continues until the teacher's turn ends or a different code is used. If a teacher response cannot be coded (e.g., an unclear or partially audible statement, a remark unrelated to the mathematics lesson (conversation with the office on the intercom), then a "no code" is used. Using a coding table of these categories and subcategories with examples, coders first reach consensus on a subset of transcripts and then code remaining transcripts independently to establish interrater reliability (e.g., Cohen's kappa of .60 or higher, approximately 80% agreement). Finally, proportions of codes are computed for each classroom by lesson and then across all lessons. These proportions become the instructional discourse patterns used when comparing classrooms (see Table 1 as an example from a nine-teacher study).

TABLE 1
Percentages for Instructional Discourse Across All Lessons in All Observed Classrooms.

	Understanding and Autonomy[a]		*Motivation, Emotion, and Social Collaboration*	
Classroom	*Supportive*	*Nonsupportive*	*Supportive*	*Nonsupportive*
Robinson	47% (19%)	9%	23%	1%
Davis	37% (13%)	19%	20%	1%
Guthrie	39% (9%)	18%	18%	2%
Christian	44% (8%)	18%	11%	5%
Hayes	28% (5%)	24%	10%	2%
Anderson	50% (24%)	13%	8%	1%
Marks	29% (10%)	32%	7%	2%
Weber	44% (13%)	24%	7%	5%
Parsons	34% (8%)	33%	6%	4%

[a]Percentages in parentheses indicate proportion of total supportive discourse coded as support for student autonomy.

THE CASE OF MRS. ROBINSON'S CLASSROOM

One of the most important contributions of qualitative research is its rich description about *how* teachers and students might create different learning contexts (Turner & Meyer, 1999). The instructional discourse patterns in Table 1 reflect very unique classroom contexts, although all nine sixth-grade teachers were using the same instructional materials and objectives. The illustrative case we have chosen is that of one of the nine observed teachers, Mrs.[1] Robinson, an African-American teacher with 22 years of elementary teaching experience. Her class of 24 sixth graders (14 females, 10 males) represented average achievement on standardized tests and were diverse in their ethnic and racial backgrounds (12 African Americans, 10 Whites, 1 Asian, and 1 Hispanic).

Mrs. Robinson's Discourse Patterns

As Table 1 illustrates, Mrs. Robinson's overall discourse pattern could be characterized as more scaffolded than nonscaffolded. She negotiated and transferred responsibility frequently and responded in highly supportive ways. Although all the teachers negotiated understanding with students, only one teacher transferred responsibility more than Mrs. Robinson. Furthermore, whereas Mrs. Robinson's discourse pattern reflected consistency in scaffolding or co-regulating with students, other teachers' discourse patterns showed greater reliance on teacher control and telling students generally what to do.

[1]We use the title of "Mrs." because that is the teacher's preferred way of making reference to herself. All names are pseudonyms.

We believe that Mrs. Robinson's discourse patterns illustrate the complex social processes that support opportunities for and development of self-regulation. Through discourse excerpts from one lesson, we highlight four types of interactions that support student self-regulation through scaffolded discourse practices: (a) establishing a supportive classroom climate, (b) building competence and maintaining a focus on learning, (c) providing opportunities for developing autonomy, and (d) supporting self-regulatory processes through shared responsibility. In addition, Mrs. Robinson's students' overall ratings of their self-regulated learning strategies were the highest among the nine classrooms. For each type of interaction, we use other student survey responses to support our interpretation that Mrs. Robinson was successful in scaffolding self-regulation.

Building a Supportive Classroom Climate

Mrs. Robinson's elementary classroom is an example of the multiple ways in which students may realize self-regulatory skills through participation in positive instructional environments (Paris & Paris, 2001). A supportive context, which can be heard woven throughout Mrs. Robinson's discourse, is important for the risks of the hard work of learning math during whole-class lessons. Mrs. Robinson's discourse analysis revealed that she had the highest proportions of socioemotional support among the nine classrooms (see Table 1). Her students rated teacher support as significantly higher than all other classrooms, except that of Ms. Davis, who had the second highest proportions of supportive motivational and socioemotional discourse.

During a lesson on November 18th, the class was at the beginning of a unit on factoring and their understanding appeared sketchy. Mrs. Robinson had confirmed the general confusion around the concept of a factor tree after walking around to check off homework. Therefore, she began class by reminding students of the purpose of homework and, moreover, of learning (coded as motivational and socioemotional supports):

MR: I talked to a few of you this morning and I could tell that there was a lot of confusion over the homework. Jewel attempted to do the homework, and she couldn't do 1 through 6, but she went ahead and did 21 through 22. And she was really upset and I told her that I was not going to penalize her because she at least ATTEMPTED to do the work. And she said, "Mrs. Robinson, you explained it on the board and I still couldn't do it and my Aunt Rita couldn't do it as well." But what is the purpose of us trying to do the homework? Amy?

Amy: Learn how to do it.

MR: Right. After I teach you the skills, that's why you do the homework, to see if you can understand the skills. Those children that don't care, which I don't have any children like that, (she speaks to the class as if confiding in them) but you know those CHILDREN—I'm sure you've HEARD of them —that don't even TRY to do their homework—but you guys, you really do TRY and that is the whole purpose of it, OK? So if you are trying to do it, just tell me, or maybe have your parents on your assignment sheet write down that we tried and couldn't do it, or something like that. OK, let's review what we did yesterday. Maybe this will clear some of the questions that you have before we go into checking our homework.

Building Competence and Focusing on Understanding

The importance of building a positive classroom climate is to provide a basis for student participation and development of self-regulation. As Yowell and Smylie (1999) explained, "when one considers the development of self-regulation within school settings, the interpersonal relations between the student and the teacher are among the most relevant variables" (p. 471). However, they go on to conclude that "although personal relationships afford for internalization—without goal achievement, they offer little" (p. 481). Instructional support that negotiates meaning, building a shared understanding of what is known and what is knowable, is necessary to promote student competence. Mrs. Robinson's students reported significantly lower use of self-handicapping strategies and feelings of negative affect after failure than students in most other classes, indicating that they approached learning with some confidence.

To build a common ground for understanding at the beginning of the lesson, Mrs. Robinson asks the students to generate all the ways the text authors might have factored the example of 100 in their textbook (e.g., 2 × 50, 4 × 25, 5 × 20, etc.). Then she carefully broke the textbook example down into steps on the overhead projector.

MR: Now let's look [at the example in the book]. Here they took the number 100 and they broke it down into a factor tree. But they used, they started off with the factors 2 times 50 (*teacher points to overhead*) and then they broke it down further into 2 times, and then they broke 50 into 25 times 2. And then they broke it down further. They brought the 2 back down, they brought this 2 down over here. What did they do with the 25, class?

Student: Broke it down into 5 times 5.

MR: And look at this, are these the same numbers that are over here? (*Comparing the factorizations of both 20 times 5 and another*) What kind of numbers are these, Charlie?

Student: Prime numbers.

MR: They are prime numbers. And usually when you break that factor tree down into the prime numbers, all prime numbers, you are do—you're what?

Student: Through.

MR: You're done, you're through. Finished. Hopefully. OK? Now, who didn't understand this part? (*Not much re-*

sponse from class—only one hand goes up. So teacher tries to encourage them, teasing.) "Oh, Mrs. Robinson, this is easy, we went over this in class. It's only when you give us different numbers." Let's go back and finish reviewing.

Building Autonomy

Self-regulation involves the process of assuming responsibility, which becomes contingent not only on the classroom climate and growing competence, but also on the opportunities afforded to demonstrate that competence. Mrs. Robinson's students, significantly more than students in most other classes, reported that their teacher had high expectations, which we interpret as an indicator of their ability to take responsibility. Once she had established that students understood the text example, Mrs. Robinson began the common practice of asking students to demonstrate their solutions at the overhead. These demonstrations shifted more of the responsibility for teaching and learning to the students by providing opportunities for students to demonstrate competence and to evaluate.

In the following example, Brittany has factored 180 and Mrs. Robinson transferred responsibility by asking her to explain the factor tree and to evaluate her solution.

MR: Right. OK, explain it to us, Brittany.

Brittany: I factored 30 and 6 and I factored 30 into 5 times 6, and I factored 6 into 2 times 3, and I took the 5 down, and I factored [the other] 6 into 3 times 2. ...

MR: What? You brought [the 2] straight down. And how do you know you are done?

Brittany: 'Cause they're all prime.

However, when Mrs. Robinson attempted to transfer responsibility to Jewel for modeling another factor tree for 180, she found that Jewel could not yet assume responsibility. Therefore, Mrs. Robinson scaffolded by suggesting a strategy for choosing the initial two factors, which Jewel was successful at using and got her started toward solving the problem.

MR: Uh, what you are going to factor it into? (*MR writes 180 on the overhead.*)

Jewel: Ummm. (*Pause*) I don't know.

MR: Want somebody to help you out? Well, how would you do it if you were at home?

Jewel: Ummm. (*Jewel is thinking.*)

MR: Get a calculator or a piece of paper?

Jewel: Umm, paper.

MR: OK, let's go. Start writing factors ... of 180. Start with 1 over here like I showed you, and then over here on the far end, what are you going to put?

Mrs. Robinson's support of Jewel required the negotiation of the simplest of concepts and skills. At the same time, she had to give support only as needed, allowing Jewel to be accountable for her understanding and earning credit for her own progress.

MR: So, what are you going to break [180] up [into]?

Jewel: To 60 and 3?

MR: OK, then what do you—OK, go ahead.

Sharing Responsibility for Learning

Mrs. Robinson's scaffolding with Jewel in this lesson evolved into an example of shared responsibility by the entire class. As the transcript unfolds, Jewel's efforts and struggles were supported by the teacher in the beginning and then increasingly by her classmates. A great deal of the difficulty that Jewel had in factoring was with the "mechanical" aspects of the factor tree. Like other areas of math, the physical organization and the sequence of steps for factoring was important to arriving at the solution.

MR: OK, keep your symbols, keep everything coming down. Okay. Now that's right, but let me tell you what you do first. Always bring that first number down, even if you cannot use it, because if not, you are going to get confused and leave it behind. Good job.

MR: Um hmm. Is she right so far? (*To class*) Is she doing a good job?

Class: YES.

MR: UH! (*Hinting at a mistake*)

Jewel: (*To class*) It's wrong, ain't it? Tell me the truth, people. (*Jewel stands and looks at the class, raises her hands as if pleading*)

Jewel: (*In a trusting but hushed voice*) Help me out, then.

MR: (*To class*) Raise your hand. (*To Jewel*) And answer, say, "What did I do wrong? Did I do anything wrong?" Well, call on somebody. (*Jewel calls on Linda.*)

Linda: You need to break down 4.

Then, Jewel initiates her own request for help:

Jewel: Should I bring the 3 down too?

MR: I don't know! (*To class*) Listen, should she bring the 3 down?

Jewel: Yes! (*She brings the 3 down.*)

MR: Go back and look at your—

One student says: There you go. (*There are sounds of students coaching her—sounds supportive. The class breaks into applause. Jewel continues. The class applauds again.*)

MR: Stay there, now, how can you write a shortened form of that? Five times 3 times 2 times 2 times 3, using exponents? (*To class*) Shhh. We did this yesterday.

Jewel: OK.
MR: (*Softly*) Remember?
Students respond in a tone: Yes! (*Class applauds.*)
MR: Equals what?
(*Jewel writes* $2^2 \times 3^2 \times 5 = 180$. *Class applauds.*)

As the excerpt illustrates, the students were actively engaged in learning how to factor numbers using factor trees. The students' ratings of the promotion of interaction in their classroom were significantly higher than all other classrooms. We saw these highly interactive whole-group lessons as evidencing co-regulation and shared responsibility as was illustrated in this instructional sequence. Although there were shifts in responsibility for demonstrating how to factor, everyone, not only the teacher, was continuously monitoring and evaluating understanding, which further promotes the development of student self-regulation. In addition, students assumed responsibility for a peer's emotional *and* cognitive support. Her peers provided support as necessary, but Jewel was the one who demonstrated her competence through assuming responsibility for explaining how to factor 180. Mrs. Robinson continued to provide supports for all the students' understanding and autonomy, but she withdrew her central position in instruction as the lesson progressed and she shared teaching and learning with her students. Jewel's success was both an individual and class success.

REFLECTIONS ON DISCOURSE ANALYSIS

Discourse analysis is a laborious and evolving research methodology. With each new set of instructional discourse patterns, we also acquire new challenges to our research questions and methods. Every classroom presents discourse practices that we must assimilate into the coding scheme or accommodate the coding scheme to reflect. Because discourse analysis allows us to test theory in classrooms while inviting practice to inform theory, our rewards have been worth the efforts.

One of the major advantages of discourse analysis is that it allows researchers to capture very complex episodes across several classroom instructional contexts. Our research findings have been richer because of the variety of classrooms in which we have been privileged to observe. For example, in our most recent work, discourse analyses helped to reveal the emotional components of mastery goals (Turner et al., in press) and the importance of cognitive *and* socioemotional supports for motivation to learn (Turner, Meyer, Midgley, & Patrick, in press). The case of Mrs. Robinson was essential to both of these findings, but it would not have been as instructive without the accompanying discourse patterns of her eight colleagues.

At the same time, we continue to face challenges to refine and improve our research methods. For example, we have not advanced our current coding scheme to simultaneously code and analyze student responses. However, we constantly are aware of the significant contributions that students make to classroom instruction that are not being captured. For example, students ask a variety of questions and they evoke their own forms of motivational and socioemotional supports through their statements of encouragement and frustration, jokes, and instructional suggestions. Capturing these student contributions to scaffolded and nonscaffolded instruction are important markers of student self-regulation that we are trying to find ways to explore more fully.

FUTURE DIRECTIONS FOR EXAMINING SRL THROUGH QUALITATIVE METHODS

Researching the complexities of classroom interactions requires contextualized theories and methods that will keep teaching and learning unified. Self-regulated learning traditionally has been examined from an individualistic perspective as externally influenced by environmental factors, but it can be viewed as a social process, implicitly binding individuals and their social contexts. Thus, it is important for educational researchers to investigate constructs like self-regulation from different theoretical perspectives and examine them with different research methodologies. A sociocultural perspective, which provides a framework for constructs like scaffolding and supports methodologies like discourse analyses, can help to explain self-regulation in compelling ways. But first, educational psychology must move beyond the historical underpinnings that ignore the social contexts of classrooms (McCaslin & Hickey, 2001a).

In conclusion, we believe that the power behind theories that fit well with practice stems from their inherent assumptions about *reciprocity* and the importance of *context* in understanding human learning and motivation. We also believe that a long overlooked aspect of the context is that of socioemotional support. The cognitive, metacognitive, and motivational processes in self-regulation are intertwined in social and emotional relationships. Thus, integrating "context" into conceptualizations of self-regulation will expand it theoretically and will challenge researchers to explore methods that bring contextualized understanding to educational research and practices.

ACKNOWLEDGMENTS

Research findings presented in this article are part of work supported by the Spencer Foundation (Grant 199800210) to Julianne C. Turner, University of Notre Dame, and Carol Midgley, University of Michigan.

We thank two anonymous reviewers for their insights and suggestions for revision of the manuscript.

The findings and opinions expressed here do not necessarily reflect the position or policies of the Spencer Foundation.

REFERENCES

Alvermann, D. E., & Hayes, D. A. (1989). Classroom discussion of content area reading assignments: An intervention study. *Reading Research Quarterly, 24,* 305–335.

Anderman, L. H., & Anderman, E. M. (Eds.). (2000). The role of social context in educational psychology: Substantive and methodological issues [Special edition]. *Educational Psychologist, 35,* 67–68.

Blumenfeld, P. C., & Meece, J. L. (1988). Task factors, teacher behavior, and students' involvement and use of learning strategies in science. *Elementary School Journal, 88,* 235–250.

Bronfenbrenner, U. (1979). *The ecology of human development: Experiments by nature and design.* Cambridge, MA: Harvard University Press.

Brophy, J. (1999). Research on motivation in education: Past, present, and future. In T. C. Urdan (Ed.), *Advances in motivation and achievement* (Vol. 11, pp. 1–44). Stamford, CT: JAI.

Greeno, J. G., Collins, A. M., & Resnick. L. B. (1996). Cognition and learning. In D. C. Berliner & R. C. Calfee (Eds.), Handbook of educational psychology (pp. 15–46). New York: Simon & Schuster Macmillan.

Hicks, D. (1996). Discourse, learning, and teaching. In M. W. Apple (Ed.), *Review of research in education, 21* (pp. 49–95). Washington, DC: American Educational Research Association.

McCaslin, M., & Good, T. L. (1996). The informal curriculum. In D. C. Berliner & R. C. Calfee (Eds.), *Handbook of educational psychology* (pp. 622–670). New York: Simon & Schuster Macmillan.

McCaslin, M., & Hickey, D. T. (2001a). Educational psychology, social constructivism, and educational practice: A case of emergent identity. *Educational Psychologist, 36,* 133–140.

McCaslin, M., & Hickey, D. T. (2001b). Self-regulated learning and academic achievement: A Vygotskian view. In B. J. Zimmerman & D. H. Schunk (Eds.), *Self-regulated learning and academic achievement: Theoretical perspectives* (pp. 227–252). Mahwah, NJ: Lawrence Erlbaum Associates, Inc.

Meece, J. L. (1991). The classroom context and students' motivational goals. In P. Pintrich & M. L. Maehr (Eds.), *Advances in motivation and achievement: Vol. 7. Goals and self-regulatory processes* (pp. 261–286). Greenwich, CT: JAI.

Mehan, H. (1985). The structure of classroom discourse. In T. van Dijk (Ed.), *Handbook of discourse analysis* (Vol. 3, pp. 119–131). London: Academic.

Paris, S. G., Byrnes, J. P., & Paris, A. H. (2001). Constructing theories, identifies, and actions of self-regulated learners. In B. J. Zimmerman & D. H. Schunk (Eds.), *Self-regulated learning and academic achievement: Theoretical perspectives* (pp. 253–288). Mahwah, NJ: Lawrence Erlbaum Associates, Inc.

Paris, S. G., & Paris, A. H. (2001). Classroom applications of research on self-regulated learning. *Educational Psychologist, 36,* 89–102.

Patrick, H., Anderman, L. H., Ryan, A. M., Edelin, K. C., & Midgley, C. (2001). Teachers' communication of goal orientations in four fifth-grade classrooms. *Elementary School Journal, 102,* 35–58.

Perry, N., & VandeKamp, K. O. (2000). Creating classroom contexts that support young children's development of self-regulated learning. *International Journal of Educational Research, 33,* 821–843.

Pintrich, P. R. (2000). The role of goal orientation in self-regulated learning. In M. Boekaerts, P. R. Pintrich, & M. Zeidner (Eds.), *Handbook of self-regulation: Theory, research, and applications* (pp. 452–502). San Diego, CA: Academic.

Rogoff, B. (1990). *Apprenticeship in thinking: Cognitive development in social context.* New York: Oxford University Press.

Schunk, D. H., & Zimmerman, B. J. (1996). Modeling and self-efficacy influences on children's development of self-regulation. In J. Juvonen & K. R. Wentzel (Eds.), *Social motivation: Understanding children's school adjustments* (pp. 154–179). New York: Cambridge University Press.

Stipek, D., Salmon, J. M., Givvin, K. B., Kazemi, E., Saxe, G., & MacGyvers, V. L. (1998). The value (and convergence) of practices suggested by motivation research and promoted by mathematics education reformers. *Journal for Research in Mathematics Education, 29,* 465–488.

Turner, J. C. (1995). The influence of classroom contexts on young children's motivation for literacy. *Reading Research Quarterly, 30,* 410–441.

Turner, J. C., & Meyer, D. K. (1999). Integrating classroom context into motivation theory and research. In T. C. Urdan (Ed.), *Advances in motivation and achievement: The role of context* (Vol. 11, pp. 87–121). Stamford, CT: JAI.

Turner, J. C., Meyer, D. K., Midgley, C., & Patrick, H. (in press). Teacher discourse and students' affect and achievement-related behaviors in two high mastery/high performance classrooms. *Elementary School Journal.*

Turner, J. C., Midgley, C., Meyer, D. K., Gheen, M., Anderman, E., Kang, J., & Patrick, H. (in press). The classroom environment and students' reports of avoidance strategies in mathematics: A multi-method study. *Journal of Educational Psychology.*

Urdan, T. C. (Ed.). (1999). *Advances in motivation and achievement: The role of context, Vol. 11.* Stamford, CT: JAI.

Vygotsky, L. S. (1978). *Mind in society: The development of higher psychological processes.* Cambridge, MA: Harvard University Press.

Weiner, B. (1996). Foreword. In J. Juvonen & K. R. Wentzel (Eds.), *Social motivation: Understanding children's school adjustments* (pp. xiii-xv). New York: Cambridge University Press.

Wood, D., Bruner, J. S., & Ross, G. (1976). The role of tutoring in problem solving. *Journal of Child Psychology and Psychiatry, 17,* 89–100.

Yowell, C. M., & Smylie, M. A. (1999). Self-regulation in democratic communities. *Elementary School Journal, 99,* 469–490.

Zimmerman, B. J. (1989). Models of self-regulated learning and academic achievement. In B. J. Zimmerman & D. H. Schunk (Eds.), *Self-regulated learning and academic achievement: Theory, research, and practice* (pp. 1–26). New York: Springer-Verlag.

Zimmerman, B. J. (2001). Theories of self-regulated learning and academic achievement: An overview and analysis. In B. J. Zimmerman & D. H. Schunk (Eds.), *Self-regulated learning and academic achievement: Theoretical perspectives* (pp. 1–38). Mahwah, NJ: Lawrence Erlbaum Associates, Inc.

Zimmerman, B. J., & Schunk, D. H. (Eds.). (2001). *Self-regulated learning and academic achievement: Theoretical perspectives.* Mahwah, NJ: Lawrence Erlbaum Associates, Inc.

EDUCATIONAL PSYCHOLOGIST, *37*(1), 27–39

Turning the Kaleidoscope: What We See When Self-Regulated Learning is Viewed With a Qualitative Lens

Helen Patrick
Department of Educational Studies
Purdue University

Michael J. Middleton
Department of Education
University of New Hampshire

This article argues for using multiple methods to investigate self-regulated learning because only by using a range of methodologies will we be able to appreciate fully its complexity. The article focuses on 2 aspects that are afforded by the use of observations and interviews in self-regulated learning research: (a) providing rich, contextualized description that can answer "what, how, why, and when" questions, and (b) enabling methodological triangulation. This article discusses these with reference to the ongoing mixed-method research of middle-grade urban students' engagement in project-based science. The article also reflects on issues and questions that have evolved throughout this research.

Self-regulated learning involves students' ability and propensity to be "active participants in their own learning" (Zimmerman, 1994, p. 3). Because it is a critical factor for students' learning and achievement, self-regulated learning has become an important area of research in educational psychology. Self-regulated learning encompasses a constellation of components, including "hot" (motivational & affective) and "cold" (cognitive & metacognitive) aspects of students' engagement in academic tasks (e.g., Pintrich & Garcia, 1991; Zimmerman, 1989). Accordingly, when researchers investigate self-regulated learning they consider cognitive, metacognitive, and motivational perceptions and behaviors. Some researchers (e.g., McCaslin & Good, 1996; Paris, Byrnes, & Paris, 2001; Pressley, 1995) note that self-regulated learning also involves a social aspect that includes interactions with peers and teachers. Positive interactions and features of the classroom environment can support students' individual efforts to engage cognitively, metacognitively, and motivationally in classroom tasks—a process that McCaslin and Good (1996) call co-regulated learning. Teachers can facilitate co-regulated learning by building social supports within the classroom, such as through creating opportunities for collaboration among peers on tasks.

Researchers typically conceptualize self-regulated learning as an aptitude—"a relatively enduring attribute of a person that predicts future behavior" (Winne & Perry, 2000, p. 534). They have tended to ask quantitative research questions and measure self-regulated learning with self-report surveys. Survey methods have produced significant advances in the understanding of self-regulated learning. They are also efficient; surveys are economical in terms of labor, relatively fast and inexpensive to administer and score, and the ensuing research has shown consistent findings among constructs. Because surveys typically require respondents to average across situations or occasions, this methodology is particularly oriented toward the stability of perceptions and behaviors. It also emphasizes generalizability to populations (Denzin, 1978). Accordingly, survey approaches to investigating self-regulated learning are compatible with implicit assumptions that the constructs reside within the individual and are relatively stable, and they de-emphasize contextual and temporal variability.

Despite its utility, an overreliance on survey methods may obscure other perspectives of self-regulated learning. For example, research within educational psychology has pointed to the importance of factors such as the nature of learning tasks, instructional contexts, and interaction for students'

Requests for reprints should be sent to Helen Patrick, Department of Educational Studies, Purdue University, 1446 LAEB, Room 5122, West Lafayette, IN 47907–1446. E-mail: hpatrick@purdue.edu

self-regulated learning. Taking these aspects into account implies also viewing self-regulated learning as a series of events, each one bounded temporally and contextually embedded (Winne & Perry, 2000). Research from an event perspective focuses on individuals' engagement in specific activities, rather than averaged across multiple occasions. This line of research demands using research methods with a focus on producing rich description.

Methods have been likened to a kaleidoscope; "depending on how they are approached, held, and acted toward, different observations will be revealed" (Denzin, 1978, pp. 292–293). Different methodologies have different assumptions, emphases, priorities, and strengths and weaknesses, and accordingly they reveal different aspects of "reality." We agree with those (e.g., Brewer & Hunter, 1989; Tashakkori, & Teddlie, 1998) who argue that one method is not inherently superior to another, but each has the potential to provide different types of information and answer different kinds of research questions. Reliance on any one method implies that researchers will continue viewing the constructs of interest from the same angle. By using a range of methods, however, researchers can consider evidence from new perspectives, giving the opportunity for previously obscured facets to be illuminated. Such is the case for understanding self-regulated learning.

Qualitative methods are particularly well-suited for examining self-regulated learning as events because they involve rich, holistic descriptions, emphasize the social settings in which the phenomena are embedded, do not make assumptions about intra-individual stability, and are oriented to revealing complexity (Brewer & Hunter, 1989; Denzin, 1978; Miles & Huberman, 1994). Two important qualitative methods are observations and interviews. Observational research is useful because it can portray learners' actions rather than their recollections or beliefs, can document how patterns of student engagement in academic tasks unfold over time, and is sensitive to the environment in which the events occur (Winne & Perry, 2000). However, observations are limited to examination of behaviors and provide limited insight into how individuals make sense of events. Open-ended interviews may complement observations because they allow respondents to reveal and explain events and experiences in their own words and from their own perspectives. Consequently, interviews enable researchers to take a grounded, inductive approach to understanding students' thoughts and behaviors, rather than only imposing their theoretical perspective or pre-established categories on what students say.

In this article we focus on two aspects that are afforded by the use of observations and interviews in self-regulated learning research: (a) providing rich, contextualized description that can answer "what, how, why, and when" questions, and (b) enabling methodological triangulation. We discuss these with reference to our ongoing mixed-method research of middle-grade urban students' cognitive, metacognitive, motivational, and collaborative engagement in inquiry-based science. We also reflect on issues and questions that have evolved throughout this research. First, however, we provide a brief description of project-based science (PBS)—the instructional context of our research, which differs in important ways from traditional classroom instruction.

OVERVIEW OF PROJECT-BASED SCIENCE

Recommendations in the last few years (American Association for the Advancement of Science, 1993; National Research Council, 1996) call for students to engage in the activities of science—asking questions, conducting investigations, collecting data, interpreting results, and reporting findings (Lunetta, 1997; Roth, 1995). Project-based science (PBS) is one of several programs that emphasize inquiry and are consistent with social constructivist learning theories (Blumenfeld, Marx, Patrick, Krajcik, & Soloway, 1997). PBS is characterized by (1) a driving question, (2) investigations, (3) artifact development, (4) collaboration among students, teacher, and others in the community, and (5) use of technology tools to support inquiry (Krajcik, Blumenfeld, Marx, & Soloway, 1994; Singer, Marx, Krajcik, & Chambers, 2000).

By using a "driving question" that contextualizes scientific ideas in the lives of the learners, the PBS curricula make inquiry authentic and intellectually worthwhile. Examples of those questions are "Why do I need to wear a helmet when I ride my bike?" (forces and motion) and "What affects the quality of air in my community?" (Air quality; see Singer et al., 2000, for description). In the process of exploring answers to the question, students encounter and come to understand scientific ideas. The curriculum begins by providing a common experience which students can refer to during the course of the project, serving to anchor their learning experiences. Students engage in inquiry by raising questions, designing investigations, apparatus, and data collection procedures, gathering and analyzing data, and presenting results. Each curriculum incorporates technology tools (e.g., modeling programs, probe software, data visualization programs) that are most appropriate for aiding inquiry as students find solutions to questions (Marx, Blumenfeld, Krajcik, & Soloway, 1997; Singer et al., 2000). Students collaborate within their groups and with others outside the classroom. Throughout the curriculum students generate artifacts, which enables them to develop and demonstrate their knowledge and allows teachers to assess the students' understanding.

The features of PBS make it a particularly interesting and relevant pedagogical environment in which to examine self-regulated learning. To exercise optimal self-regulated learning, students need opportunities for being reflective and for integrating knowledge and experiences. They also benefit from motivationally rich curricula that contain inherently interesting and meaningful content, with opportunities for choice and control, which will provoke and sustain effortful cognitive and metacognitive engagement (Ryan & Stiller,

1991; Zimmerman, 1994). These opportunities for students to be self-regulated, rather than other-regulated, are not always plentiful in traditional classrooms. PBS encourages students to be cognitively and metacognitively engaged. They are asked to consider multiple reference points for science concepts (e.g., real life applications, investigations). They are expected to think systematically and deeply about the questions proposed (e.g., designing experiments, creating and testing hypotheses, building and testing computer models). For example, students use software to create models of pollution sources, effects of pollution, and directional relationships among pollutants and effects (Jackson, Stratford, Krajcik, & Soloway, 1994). This helps students to connect different pieces that they have learned and think about how the pieces fit together to answer the driving question. Students are required to represent their own ideas in multiple ways (e.g., verbal presentations, graphs and charts, computer models). PBS is also designed to facilitate students' intrinsic motivation. Important objectives of PBS curricula are to make connections between the science content and the real world, so that students will appreciate the relevance of learning science, and to stimulate interest in science issues so that students will continue to think about them outside the classroom (Blumenfeld et al., 1991). By allowing students to explore questions of importance in their lives and to their communities, it is expected that they will be motivated to engage deeply in the process of doing and learning science. Finally, students are required to collaborate with peers during tasks. Successful inquiry demands that students pay attention to their work to explain their ideas, justify their actions, and cooperate with others. Thus, success in PBS requires the cognitive, metacognitive, motivational, and collaborative engagement that comprises self-regulated learning. Optimally, therefore, students in PBS classes will have opportunities to be self-regulated in their learning, and those classes will be rich contexts for researchers to investigate this process.

Method

We illustrate some of the benefits of using qualitative measures of self-regulated learning with our research involving urban seventh- and eighth-grade students engaged in PBS. This research is part of our ongoing work with the National Science Foundation-funded Center for Learning Technologies in Urban Schools, the Chicago and Detroit Urban Systemic Initiatives in Science, and support from the Spencer Foundation. This research focuses on creating additional inquiry-based science curricula (Singer et al., 2000), supporting teachers in using these curricula (Fishman, Best, Foster, & Marx, 2000), investigating how students and teachers engage with the science (Patrick, Middleton, & Taines, 2000; Taines, Schneider, & Blumenfeld, 2000), and making iterative curricular changes (Blumenfeld, Fishman, Krajcik, Marx, & Soloway, 2000). Almost all the participating students from Detroit were African American, whereas students in Chicago were ethnically diverse (e.g., Eastern European, Middle Eastern, Central American) and most spoke a language other than English at home. Within each science class we focused particularly on a subsample of 4–5 students for more intensive study. These "target students" were nominated by the teacher based on criteria of good attendance, average achievement level, and anticipated willingness to share their thoughts. Seventh graders used water-quality and air-quality curricula, and eighth graders used curricula about global warming (Edelson, Gordin, & Pea, 1999) and about force and motion. Classes spent approximately 10 weeks on a curriculum, although there was wide variability.

A range of methods was used to examine different facets of students' self-regulated learning, in addition to their learning and achievement: classroom observations, interviews, and self-report surveys. Classroom observations were conducted by videotaping target classrooms approximately three times per week over the course of the curriculum. Videographers focused on teachers' presentation of lessons, students' engagement in inquiry projects and use of technology, and whole-class and small-group discussions. The focus was on at least one of the target students and his or her group. We later created a detailed summary of each videotape, including descriptions of teacher and student behavior and conversations. From these observations we noted instances when students responded in ways that indicated they were engaged cognitively, metacognitively, motivationally, or collaboratively—such as when they appeared from their talk or behavior to be thoughtful, strategic, reflective, involved, interested, or interactive.

At the end of the curriculum unit researchers conducted individual 20–30 minute interviews with target students to investigate their attitudes, beliefs, and perceptions about science in general and about their experiences during the science curriculum. The interviewers followed a protocol of open-ended questions and encouraged the students to give explanations and examples as illustration. The questions referred to the driving question (e.g., if and how it related to the real world, to the investigations, and to the presentation), students' cognitive and metacognitive engagement (e.g., the kinds of things they thought about, how they went about learning what they needed), motivation (e.g., whether learning about science is interesting and is useful, what part of PBS they enjoyed the most, whether they talked with others or read about science outside the classroom), collaboration (e.g., whether they discussed their ideas with others, liked working in a group, whether working with others helped them learn science,), and technology use (e.g., how the technology fitted with what they were learning).

Self-report surveys of attitudes and beliefs about science were administered to all students participating in the curricula. Well-established measures, including use of cognitive and metacognitive strategies (Pintrich, Smith, Garcia, & McKeachie, 1993), motivation (Midgley et al., 1996), and perceived collaborative support (Taylor, Fraser, & Fisher, 1997) were adapted to match the curricula. Items were factor analyzed and separate scales were created.

All the aforementioned data sources are able to contribute to our understanding of students' self-regulated learning. Each method type can answer different kinds of questions or afford a different view of self-regulated learning.

PROVIDING CONTEXTUALIZED DESCRIPTION: ANSWERING WHAT, HOW, WHY, AND WHEN QUESTIONS

Quantitative approaches to self-regulated learning generally ask questions about frequency, such as "how much?" or "how often?" Although important, they are not the only questions that researchers and practitioners need answers to. Paris et al. (2001) argued recently that our views that student learning is situated and socially constructed have implications for how we consider self-regulated learning. That is, within a social constructivist framework "the actions to be regulated and the goals to be pursued are specified by particular social roles and situations" (Paris et al., 2001, p. 255). Accordingly, we also need to ask "the what, how, why, and when questions surrounding SRL" (p. 255) that include the context and students' personal histories. Similarly, others (e.g., Hickey, 1997; Paris & Turner, 1994; Turner & Meyer, 1999) have argued for the need to take a situated or contextualized view of motivation to answer these same kinds of questions.

Consistent with these recent conceptualizations of self-regulated learning and motivation as being situationally constructed and consistent with our experiences investigating students engaged in PBS, these "what, how, why, and when" questions emerged as central within our research. Accordingly, we realized that we needed to use qualitative and mixed-method approaches when answering our research questions. Qualitative methods such as observations and interviews are contextually sensitive and afford "thick," vivid description (Miles & Huberman, 1994) and so they are ideal for addressing "what, how, why, and when" questions. We can learn much about students' self-regulated learning from rich descriptions of students and their surroundings, constructed after having observed them engaged in academic tasks, and from asking them about their understandings and reasoning related to that engagement. For example, we can learn from observations how students go about engaging in complex academic tasks, what they talk about, how they explain concepts to others, how typical and optimal patterns of engagement differ qualitatively, and under what circumstances optimal cognitive and motivational engagement appear to be elicited. From interviews we can appreciate students' understanding of the task and other requirements, learn the kinds of things they think about during and after engaging in activities, what aspects of the task and context they think encourage and support their persistence and thoughtfulness, and why they do what they do.

In the following section we discuss the kinds of questions we reflected on while observing students and interviewing them about their cognitive, metacognitive, motivational, and collaborative engagement in PBS. We argue that this information is important to enhance our view of students' self-regulated learning.

What are Students Being Metacognitive About?

One question that warrants consideration involves the focus of students' cognitive and metacognitive engagement: What are they monitoring and evaluating? When the students were observed regularly during science class they appeared, almost without exception, to be engaged in the activities. In general they were attentive to, and talked about, what they and others were doing. When we considered the focus of students' attention, though, it was evident that their cognitive and metacognitive engagement was directed in large part at following procedures or at more superficial aspects of the task, rather than to understanding ideas (Taines et al., 2000). This was evident also during students' construction of artifacts. Examples come from the period during the air-quality curriculum when students worked on creating posters for a group presentation about one of a range of pollutants. We observed students reflecting on and debating questions such as the color and size of the lettering or the extent of students' artistic skill, rather than ensuring that they achieved an integrated understanding of, for example, what the chemical formulae meant or how CFCs damage the ozone layer. When Toshanda explained during her interview what she liked most about the air-quality curriculum, she talked about how her group inserted comedy into their final presentation about carbon dioxide "so that it was not boring." Observations such as these suggest that we have to note the quality or target of students' engagement and not just attend to the amount. We need to question whether their metacognition is directed toward features of the tasks that will promote learning and understanding, rather than more superficial aspects of the task. It is not sufficient, however, to consider only what the students focus their thinking on, but to also note the teachers' directions—an issue we discuss in a later section.

What do Students Believe Learning Involves?

Another essential question to consider when attempting to understand students' self-regulated learning, is what their epistemological beliefs, or views about the "nature and justification of human knowledge" (Hofer & Pintrich, 1997, p. 88) are. Hofer and Pintrich have suggested that beliefs about the nature of knowledge vary along two core dimensions: its simplicity (ranging from being isolated and ambiguous pieces to being comprised of highly interrelated concepts) and its certainty (from being absolute to being uncertain and evolving).

Both of these dimensions have implications for students' self-regulated learning, particularly the kinds of learning strategies they employ (Hofer, 2001). That is, if students believe that knowledge is simple, then there is little reason for them to try to integrate different ideas and knowledge sources. Similarly, if they believe that knowledge is certain, they may be unlikely to think about exceptions or question whether there is conflicting evidence.

Our interviews with students revealed their perspectives and understandings about knowledge and learning; like most other students they seemed to view knowledge as being simple and certain. The interviews also illustrated the importance of students' beliefs about what learning and knowledge involve for their self-regulated learning. For example, our interview with Hazem pointed to associations between his views about knowledge and his cognitive and metacognitive engagement with the global-warming content. When he talked about an investigation that showed that darker colors absorb more heat than lighter colors, Hazem mentioned a question that was raised by one of his friends: Why are deserts hotter than rain forests, even though the yellow sand is a lighter color than the green vegetation of rain forests? Like many early adolescents, Hazem appeared to perceive knowledge as simple. Accordingly, he seemed to view the question as an intrusion to his learning, rather than as a prompt to integrate new and existing knowledge. He said to us, "If my friend never told me that [question], it would be a lot more easier for me to learn about the global warming." Later in the interview we got a sense that Hazem also viewed knowledge as certain. He expressed discomfort with the format of the science class in general, in which students were encouraged to think about related issues, make their own hypotheses, support them with reasons, and debate alternative and sometimes conflicting hypotheses in small groups or as a class. It appeared that he wanted facts to learn and found the emphasis on discussing alternative viewpoints distracting and obscured the identification of facts. "With science, like global warming, there's facts and there's opinions in science. When it comes to opinions, there can be lots of them so you're confused and have a lot of questions and other people might think something else and tell you and you can be quite confused." He preferred to ask a classmate next to him, who would "say things straight up. ... He will tell me in a simple way and I understand."

We may learn more about students' self-regulated learning if we also gather information about their epistemological beliefs. Educators (e.g., teachers, program developers, researchers) must actively address students' views of knowledge and learning; they can not assume that students will automatically realize that they must actively integrate and revise new and existing information.

What do Students Think Motivates Them?

Theories of achievement motivation emphasize students' personal beliefs related to academics such as interest, confidence about their ability to learn, perceived value in the task, and goal orientations (e.g., wanting to understand, wanting to demonstrate ability, not wanting to demonstrate inability). Survey research has identified that these motivational constructs are related to students' cognitive and metacognitive engagement in important ways (Pintrich & Schrauben, 1992). That is, for example, the more that students want to learn about science, believe they can, believe it will be beneficial to them, and enjoy being in their science class, the more they will engage cognitively and metacognitively with the tasks, and try and persevere—behaviors that promote their learning and understanding. Despite the utility of these theories and the supporting research, however, it may be instructive to also ask students what *they* think motivates them.

When we interviewed students about what they thought influenced their motivation regarding PBS there was considerable variability in their answers, and many of them did not fit well with the focus on academics represented in motivational theories. Students did, overwhelmingly, report that they thought the driving questions were interesting and topics were related to the real world. For example, they made comments such as "Our school walk activity showed the impact of pollution on everything," "When we learned about air pollution I kept thinking about my cousin with asthma," and "I started to see that everything moves. The [force-and-motion] project helped me learn how and why." However, other factors much less related to science content seemed to be most motivating in terms of "hooking students in" to engaging with the curriculum. For some students what was most important was the opportunity to talk and work with peers. For others, the opportunities to conduct experiments were most important for their willingness to participate. And yet others talked about the opportunities to use computers as having the greatest attraction. For example, when asked why they said they liked the curriculum, Yousra said, "Because we worked with a group and we didn't have to work individual[ly]," Gina said, "It isn't like you read about it and have to remember. With [experiments] you play around with it, explore, feel it," and Connor said, "I wouldn't want to learn on just paper and pencil. I want to learn from a computer." Even though current motivational theories are beneficial for understanding students' self-regulated learning, we believe that we can also learn from students' unconstrained comments and from attempts to align the two.

Why do Students Think Learning About Science is Valuable?

Generally, motivational theorists recommend that the use of curricula that address relevant questions and include interesting content will provoke students to want to answer questions and to understand the content. Our interviews illustrated the difficulties associated with doing so. As mentioned, it was clear that students found the curricula interesting and meaningful, and they talked typically about the relevancy of what they were learning to the world. However, they did not seem to take what they learned outside the classroom when they left. When we asked about behaviors that might signal continued motivation or thoughtfulness outside the lessons such as reading books, noticing newspaper articles, or talking to parents, students tended to say that they did not do these things. Indeed, it seemed that they often looked or sounded surprised that we asked. When students talked about the value of what they were learning, a few made comments such as, "I learned how I could help my air, since I'm young, so when I get older I can do stuff to stop my air from being polluted." Many more students, however, talked only about the value of what they were learning in terms of utility for subsequent tests or classes. For example, when Marius explained the benefit of studying global warming, he said, "It was on the Iowa's [standardized assessment], so it helped us." When Steven elaborated on why he found learning about the pollutants interesting he said, "I know all about them now and at least when I get into high school and we come back to something like this, I'll know what we'll be talking about." Serena also talked about the utility of what she and her classmates learned in terms of preparation for high school, saying, "Most kids are going to take science in high school, so then this [the global-warming curriculum] was, like, really good preparation." Thus, even though students reported perceiving value in what they were learning, the value seemed to be mostly in terms of utility—that the learning would help them get extrinsic benefits such as grades or test scores, rather than be valuable for its own sake. Investigating qualitative differences in students' motivational perceptions, such as these, will also help our understanding of their self-regulated learning.

How do Students Support Each Others' Learning?

Student interaction is an important component of curricula based on social constructivism. Collaborative small group work is frequently promoted to achieve curricular goals. Optimally, students will support each other toward becoming self-regulated, or engage in co-regulation (McCaslin & Good, 1996; McCaslin & Hickey, 2001). That is, they will monitor task engagement and each other's actions, contribute ideas, interpretations, and conclusions, develop strategic ways to approach problems, promote conceptual change and more complex understandings than can be constructed independently, and sustain involvement through encouragement and support. However there is still much to be understood about how students support each other's learning, and more description of typical and optimal instances would be helpful.

Because PBS involves considerable collaborative activities, we observed instances in which students did appear to co-regulate learning. One example comes from the global-warming curriculum. After the class conducted an investigation about colors and heat absorption, a student raised a question that he had been pondering on: Why are deserts hotter than rain forests, even though the yellow sand is a lighter color than the green vegetation of rain forests? Students spent time within several class periods discussing and debating answers to this question. In one group students each suggested their own explanation for deserts being hotter, such as there being no clouds over the desert to reflect the heat, the minerals in sand causing more sunlight to be reflected, and there being no greenhouse effect over the deserts. Marius tried to convince the others that deserts were hot because there was no greenhouse effect overhead. Danetta disagreed, saying, "There kind of has to be a greenhouse effect. I mean, there is one all around the whole earth. So why not the desert?" Marius replied, "If there is no greenhouse effect, then it's more direct sunlight. It just comes through, and it's hotter because. …" He then stopped and looked frustrated, perhaps realizing that he could not support his hypothesis and said, "I don't know." Marius and the other students together considered other hypotheses that might answer the question.

In another example, from the force-and-motion curriculum, we saw how students developed an understanding of what distance–time graphs represent by interacting with group members and technology. One activity in a series using motion probes involved students walking in different patterns (toward and away from the probes and pausing) to replicate specified distance–time graphs. The students, however, did not understand at first what the graph represented and traced a zig-zag pattern on the floor while walking toward the probe. After each trial they identified that their graph did not match the model, discussed it amongst themselves, and then retried until, after the fourth attempt, Victoria realized what the graph was indicating. She then explained the necessary sequence of walking forwards, pausing, then walking backwards to her group members. They successfully completed the task.

In both of the previous examples, students were pressed to revise their initial thoughts, and this push to resolve cognitive conflict came from peers. In addition, the encouragement from group members seemed to support students' motivation and willingness to stick with tasks that were challenging and not met with initial success. Because the students' individual contributions to the discussions were fragmented and overlapping, they would be difficult to ascribe to individuals and quantify with standard survey measures and would not be easy to average over time.

What Kinds of Difficulties Need to be Overcome to Maximize Collaborative Work?

Despite the promise of peer collaboration, not all group activities produce collaboration and positive learning outcomes. Again, descriptions of students' thoughts and behaviors can assist our understanding of processes that impact on self-regulated and co-regulated learning. Students' beliefs about collaboration are likely to influence their objectives for, and behavior in, small group activities. These beliefs are also associated with views about epistemology and students' cognitive and metacognitive engagement. During our interviews it was clear that students do not always view collaboration in ways that researchers and teachers may expect or want. For example, Toshanda said she liked working in a group because everyone had an opinion and contributed answers, therefore she would have a greater likelihood of being correct. However, her reasoning was not that group members would contribute thoughts for integration and evaluation to arrive at the best answer, but that she could collect a range of answers from the whole group and therefore would always have at least one correct answer. Grant's comments about collaboration similarly involved perceptions of its purpose and utility. He told the interviewer, "The bad thing about group work is that others like to talk. ... I work faster by myself. But, group members can be good when you need help."

During the interviews we got a vivid sense of how students sometimes find collaborative work to be difficult, and of the complex goal coordination that students engage in during school activities (see McCaslin & Hickey, 2001). For example, Marius acknowledged that working with group members helped his metacognitive awareness but indicated that it introduced affective challenges. He said,

> Before, I would always say, "No, I'm always right and I always got the right answer." But now I found out that I'm not always right and there are other people with different views, and I have to look at their view from their point of view. ... Sometimes it really got on my nerves when other people said that I was always wrong. And so I'm, like, "Fine!', you know? ... Sometimes when they all got on me I got really mad.

And Amber, in the force-and-motion unit, captured the necessary goal coordination with regard to collaboration when she said,

> It's helpful to get everyone's ideas. It clarifies things when you listen to what others have to say. ... But it's not always fun because the others don't always want to work. I just have to let others have their ideas and let them talk.

Research has indicated that without explicit teacher attention to social dynamics, patterns of student collaboration and engagement in small-group activities are often disappointing, with participation and quality of thoughtfulness typically quite uneven across students (Good, Mulryan, & McCaslin, 1992; O'Donnell & O'Kelly, 1994). There has been little research about how teachers can facilitate learning in social-constructivist-based curricula (Blumenfeld et al., 1997), and descriptions of teacher practices that do foster positive student interaction and collaboration will be helpful, particularly for teachers and curriculum developers. For example, we observed a very skilled and experienced teacher mediate a sometimes heated discussion between two students who had misconstrued each other's interactions. When Ramond disagreed with Praneeta during a small group discussion, she thought he was implying that she was not smart enough and she consequently stopped talking. He responded by expressing frustration that she was "giving up." The teacher intervened to have Ramond clarify that he wanted to debate an issue with Praneeta because he did think she was clever and he found her comments thoughtful. Together Ramond, Praneeta, and the teacher established specific interaction norms. Understanding students' perceptions regarding interaction, and addressing the collaborative context, was necessary for the students being able to continue with their learning.

As others have suggested, data from observing and interviewing students challenge the often implicit assumption that self-regulation is a solitary, individualistic construct, and illustrate that self-regulation can be promoted by peers. The data also illustrate that, even though some students report that the opportunity to work with peers is the best aspect of PBS, many students experience frustrations, and the collaborative process often must be addressed explicitly by the teacher.

How do Teachers Promote and Support Students' Self-Regulated Learning?

When investigating self-regulated learning, researchers need to look past individual students to consider the instructional context. For example, what are the norms and expectations for engagement? What is promoted in the classroom? For example, we noted in a previous section that students' thoughts and actions appeared to be focused often on procedural aspects of the tasks. However, the task procedures were what the teachers themselves tended to stress to students. These teachers, though, were in the early stages of learning to enact social-constructivist instruction—an approach that is difficult to instantiate (e.g., Putnam, Heaton, Prawat, & Remillard, 1992; Richardson & Anders, 1994). Accordingly, opportunities afforded by the curricula vary considerably by classroom while teachers learn to enact it.

Our classroom observations have allowed us to appreciate ways in which teachers may encourage or facilitate different aspects of self-regulated learning. One way they do so is through academic press, which is the academic demand for understanding or performance that the teacher places on students to engage in their classwork. Teachers differ in how they create and utilize opportunities to press students to be thoughtful and press students for understanding (Blumenfeld, 1992). In one study from our project, Middleton and Blumenfeld (2000) used observation and interview data to describe patterns of academic press for understanding that teachers used in the classroom. One teacher in the study displayed a strong press for understanding, whereas another pressed students for achievement and grades, and a third exhibited low or no press. They suggested that the type and amount of press may serve as a scaffold and mediate students' self-regulated learning.

Our understanding of students' self-regulated learning can be enriched through using observations and interviews, as we have suggested in this section. It can also be instructive to triangulate the findings from qualitative methods with results gathered from quantitative methods. In the following section we discuss a recent study in which we did attempt to integrate observation, interview, and survey data from students engaged in PBS, and we subsequently reflect on questions that arose from that study.

METHODOLOGICAL TRIANGULATION

The concept of triangulation comes from nautical and surveying practices, wherein measurements from more than one vantage point are combined to identify a location or endpoint (Tashakkori & Teddlie, 1998). In applying the process to sociological research, Denzin (1978) identified four different types of triangulation, each of which involves integrating multiple perspectives. One type is methodological triangulation, or using different forms or types of measures. This may involve comparing either measures within the same method, or across different methods. The across-method, or mixed-method, approach is often thought to be preferable, however, because it allows for the inherent weaknesses of one method to be compensated for by another (Brewer & Hunter, 1989; Denzin, 1978; Tashakkori & Teddlie, 1998). Thus, triangulation affords researchers opportunities for greater completeness with respect to answering questions, compared to a mono-method approach, and confirmation of information where data overlap (Morse, 2001).

Our use of multiple methods to investigate students' self-regulation in PBS classes afforded an opportunity to examine different aspects of self-regulated learning from various vantage points. In one study we focused on the target students for whom we had observational, interview, and survey data (Patrick et al., 2000). We conducted cluster analysis with the survey measures (use of cognitive & metacognitive strategies, personal motivational beliefs, situational interest, & collaborative support) to identify different patterns of self-regulated learning among those students. We identified five significantly different patterns of self-regulated learning. Looking at previously developed case studies, we then examined students' observed behavior patterns during science lessons and their interview responses. We were interested in discernible patterns of students' behavioral engagement; discourse indicative of strategic and metacognitive action, interest, enjoyment, and wanting to understand; and what they said about their science engagement and collaboration during the interviews. We were also interested in the extent to which these qualitative findings were congruent with their survey reports. We discuss issues of triangulation in descriptions of three seventh graders (Janelle, Steven, and Toshanda) who participated in the air-quality curriculum.

Cognition and Metacognition

The survey measure of students' use of cognitive and metacognitive learning strategies during inquiry included items about elaboration, organization, and metacognitive self-regulation. Examples include, "When I am learning science I try to make the ideas fit together," "To help me understand the things I do for science I make outlines, concept maps, or pictures," and "When doing my work in science I stop once in a while and go over what I have done." Accordingly, we expected that students who reported on the survey high levels of cognitive and metacognitive strategy use would revise their suggestions, evaluate others' comments, refer back to previous lessons, and report trying to make knowledge fit together. Janelle's survey scores placed her in a cluster characterized by very high (> 1 *SD* of all target students) use of cognitive and metacognitive strategies. We did see evidence of Janelle concentrating on what her group (with Monique and Steven) was doing and being thoughtful about how they engaged in tasks. Steven was usually the first person in the group to begin the group activity, and Janelle tended to watch and check what he did. She often noticed when he made a mistake and she corrected it, such as when he was setting up equipment or answering worksheet questions. We did not observe instances of Janelle making thoughtful comments in relating what they were doing to larger science concepts, although this was not promoted by the teacher.

Steven's cluster, although different from Janelle's, was also characterized by very high (> 1 *SD*) cognitive and metacognitive strategy scores. Although Steven was always on task during the investigations, our observations were not consistent with his survey reports. Steven routinely worked out answers very quickly, then told the other group members or offered them his paper to copy—sometimes insistently. His work was often inaccurate, however, and Janelle corrected him frequently. Nevertheless, Steven appeared undaunted by making mistakes, saying "Whoops" and making the correction. During the interview Steven admitted that there were many parts of the unit that he "did not get"; for example he said, "When we did the graphing part, I didn't get that either. But it was really interesting." Despite his apparent difficulty understanding the content, he always acted confidently during the lessons.

Toshanda's survey scores placed her in a cluster of below-average (for all target students) use of cognitive and metacognitive strategies. Accordingly, we expected that she would make few thoughtful comments regarding her group's observations and conclusions. However, we saw evidence of strategic thinking and reflection from Toshanda, despite her low report on the survey. During one whole class recitation, when group members (with Kristyna, Denise, and Vincent) gave conflicting conclusions for an experiment they had conducted together, it was Toshanda who came to the correct conclusion and convinced her teacher she was right by using evidence from the experiment. When students used software designed to help them model relationships among pollutants, their sources, and their effects, Toshanda was one of the first to think about connections between different pollutants. During the interview, Toshanda talked about how creating relationships on the computer helped her to learn because they provided visual examples of the content, even though she sometimes had trouble explaining the rationale for the connections. When she talked about liking conducting investigations, her explanations were in terms of helping her understanding:

> You can see and make observations up close. … If she [the teacher] just tells you about it then you won't get the full effect—you can't picture it in your head. But if you see it, and you do it yourself, then you really know what she's talking about. You will be able to understand it better.

Therefore, despite her low survey score, it was clear that Toshanda was being metacognitive; she was trying to visualize and integrate knowledge.

Motivation

We used two survey measures of motivation. One measure addressed students' personal motivation for science, including their personal interest and mastery goal orientation. Examples of items include, "I like learning about science" and "An important reason why I do my science work is because I want to get better at it." The second measure addressed students' situational interest and enjoyment of science class, and included items such as "I would rather be in my science class than any other one." In line with these items, we expected that students who reported high levels of personal motivation and enjoyment of science class on the survey would appear involved in activities, ask questions about content, report wanting to understand science, and report thinking about science outside class. Janelle's survey placed her in the cluster having very high (> 1 *SD*) scores on both motivation measures. Janelle appeared to be interested in science and to always enjoy science class. When her group gathered data she usually participated or watched Steven and talked with him about what they were doing. She seemed to want to be involved and found ways to participate when he was domineering. For example, after he had tested the pH of two substances Janelle asked if she could test the next one, which she did. She and Steven then continued to share testing the substances. On another occasion, when Steven had been setting up the apparatus and taking measurements, Janelle announced that they needed group consensus on what the results were and she and Monique began also taking measurements. Although appearing to enjoy science class, Janelle was not always focused on the science content; sometimes she talked with Monique about social topics or they sang or laughed together. Monique appeared clearly not interested in the tasks and usually copied from Janelle and Steven at the end of the activity. Thus, it appeared that Janelle held multiple goals for science class and successfully negotiated both task involvement and social interactions with Monique.

Steven's survey scores placed him in the cluster of above-average personal interest and mastery orientation regarding science, and very high (> 1 *SD*) enjoyment of science class. Steven expressed interest in science during the interview. He talked about how he now thinks about air quality when he sees a smoke stack or thinks about acid rain when it rains. He also expressed concern about neighborhood pollution: "Like our Detroit River water, that's polluted. And like people been throwing toxic waste all up in our water. Fishes die and everything. So, it affects the whole world basically." Consistent with his survey reports, Steven seemed to enjoy science classes immensely. He tried to assume a leadership role in his group, although Janelle and Monique did not always let him. When the group gathered data he was always enthusiastic and involved and often carried out the procedure himself. He usually positioned the experimental apparatus close to where he was sitting so he could record data conveniently. He appeared to relish having an opportunity to handle "dangerous chemicals." When Janelle, partway through an investigation, asked to test the pH of some of the substances, Steven made certain that he kept the sulfuric acid and ammonia for himself and passed the aspirin and baking soda to Janelle. Consistent with our observations, during the interview when Steven talked about what he liked most in science class he said, "The part when we started messing around with sulfuric acid and stuff in the jar" and "Fooling around with carbon monoxide and glass jars." From our observations of Steven it appeared that wanting to be perceived by others as being good at science was tremendously important to him. For example, during investigations and written tasks he often told his group members that he was smart and bragged when he made accurate predictions.

Toshanda's survey scores placed her in the cluster of below-average personal interest and mastery orientation regarding science, and very low (< 1 *SD* of all target students) enjoyment of science class. Accordingly, we expected that during the interview she would express little interest in science and show little indication of enthusiasm and enjoying class activities during the observed lessons. However, when interviewed, Toshanda said that she generally liked science, even though it was hard. She expressed interest in learning about acid rain and the ozone layer, and said she had started to think more and care about them. From our observations, Toshanda also appeared interested and engaged in the science activities. She and Kristyna were usually the most actively involved of their group, and they carried out the investigation procedures for the group together. In the interview Toshanda said that she enjoyed the opportunities for active participation in science class, such as conducting investigations and giving presentations. However, Toshanda noted that she was not doing well in science, it was not one of her best subjects, and she usually felt unprepared because she had not covered this material before.

Collaborative Support for Inquiry

The survey measure of collaborative support for inquiry referred to explaining and interacting with group members and using peers' suggestions. Examples of items include, "In science class I explain my ideas to other students," "When I work in groups in science class there is teamwork," and "I learn from other students in science class." In line with these items, we expected that students who reported high levels of collaborative support on the survey would discuss the science with other group members, share their ideas and conclusions, listen to those of others, and report liking working with group members. Janelle's survey scores placed her in a cluster characterized by very high (> 1 *SD*) collaborative support. Accordingly, we expected that she would interact frequently and share her ideas within the group. In addition to Janelle talking to Steven about what they were doing, she sometimes attempted to have the whole group involved in conducting investigations, as evidenced by her demand for group consensus as a way to force her and Monique's participation during the investigation of substances' pH. However, her interactions with Monique were typically social or involved telling her the answers or giving her the notes to copy at the end of the activity.

Steven perceived his group differently from Janelle, with his survey scores placing him in a cluster characterized by below-average collaborative support. Consistent with this, we did not observe Steven interacting collaboratively with group members during tasks. His interactions with Janelle and Monique involved predominantly telling them what to do, such as to stop singing and be more serious or to put on their safety goggles, or telling them answers or results he had generated and encouraging them to copy from him. Steven seemed to prefer to work on tasks on his own, and during the interview said he did not enjoy his group. Steven spoke of Janelle as "the queen of the table" who "would like to do everything." He blamed the two girls for making mistakes and getting their information wrong. Steven also said during the interview that he did not find discussions helpful for learning. He said, "If people explain it, people ask questions and then you'll lose track and then we won't know what we're talking about … and just talking about it, you can easily forget about it quickly."

Toshanda's survey scores placed her in a cluster of above-average collaboration. Accordingly, we expected that she would be actively engaged in discussions and sharing of ideas within her group. However, we observed little collaboration in Toshanda's group. When Toshanda set up and executed the procedures she typically placed the apparatus beside herself and Kristyna so that Vincent and Denise could not see easily. Vincent and Denise tended to be quiet during group activities unless they were all off-task and socializing. Her group did not discuss the results of investigations and form conclusions together, but made conclusions individually. These were shared for the first time during whole-class discussions and tended to be conflicting.

ONGOING ISSUES FOR CONSIDERATION

The intensive focus on individual students, gained from conducting interviews and observations of students engaged in science inquiry, added rich information to their self-report survey scores. Methodological triangulation, however, can result in tension between findings from the different methods (Morse, 2001). Indeed, our use of different methodologies raised as many questions as it seemed to answer because the observed indications of specific students' self-regulated learning were not always consistent with their reports, either in the survey or the interview. What can we make of the limited triangulation among our findings from the observations, interviews, and surveys?

Limited congruence among measures may require questioning the construct validity of one or some of the measures (Pintrich, Wolters, & Baxter, 2000). Our survey measures of cognitive and metacognitive strategy use and motivation were based on previously validated and commonly used scales (e.g., PALS, Midgley et al., 1996; MSLQ, Pintrich et al., 1993). Furthermore, we found patterns of relations among those scales consistent with what other researchers have also found (Patrick et al., 2000). Nevertheless, our findings of limited congruence among measures suggest we need to consider what students and researchers mean by the words that are used. Why, for example, did Steven report on the survey high use of cognitive and metacognitive strategies but admit in the interview that he often did not understand what was happening or what he was supposed to do, and yet he was observed displaying boundless confidence in class? How do we reconcile Toshanda's reports of low motivation for science class and our observations of her being consistently involved and active? What did Toshanda and Janelle mean by collaboration that might explain their self-reports of high collaborative support and our contradictory observations of them within their groups? It may be that researchers and students do not interpret survey questions in the same way. Perhaps middle-grade students often think of concepts such as "teamwork" in terms of group members doing separate parts of a larger task without conflict, but not necessarily with collaboration or discussion. Perhaps they consider "explaining ideas" and "learning from others" to involve one student telling the answer to another.

It may also be possible that the survey questions do not accurately reflect the tasks and expectations of more inquiry-based classrooms. Characteristics of classrooms (e.g., the curriculum, the instruction, the inquiry, and the collaborative nature of classrooms) facilitate different aspects of self-regulated learning, such as strategy use or motivation. Perhaps, as Hickey (1997) has suggested, motivation may appear very differently in classrooms that use social-constructivist pedagogy compared to classrooms researched in the past. Perhaps our typical methodological tools, which were developed in more traditional classrooms, will have difficulty capturing the essence of self-regulated learning in classrooms that utilize social-constructivist approaches and curricula. Accordingly, survey measures developed and validated in more traditional classroom settings may need to be revised to fit the nature of classroom pedagogy (Hickey, 1997). We attempted to change some items in our scales to reflect the features of PBS, but more thought in this direction may be necessary.

Another response to inconsistencies evident in triangulation may be that they signal a need for further analysis of the research questions (Brewer & Hunter, 1989). What else should we be asking? We agree with suggestions to extend the range of questions beyond those that are easily quantifiable, to incorporate questions about the situation, the target, and the quality of engagement that can be answered qualitatively. Perhaps we should be wondering less about how much students think about their work, or want to learn and understand, and more about what their assumptions are about the way they should or could be thinking and what learning and understanding involves. The descriptions of students' engagement over time in PBS and the windows into their thinking shared during interviews, together with the discrepancies with findings from survey measures, support Winne and Perry's (2000) recommendation that researchers attend more to how academic tasks are defined, and their suggestion that students' beliefs about school tasks can limit the scope and quality of their self-regulated learning. It is evident that, in investigating students' self-regulated learning, we need to take their beliefs (e.g., about epistemology, specific task requirements, collaboration) and the context (e.g., pedagogical) into account.

The interviews with students also underscore the inherent difficulties getting past students' extant beliefs that appear to limit school learning to other school contexts, even when they can articulate relevancy to the world outside school. Bereiter (1990) noted that students typically acquire a "school work module" very early in their educational careers, wherein they view learning as "knowledge telling." An important goal of PBS, as of other curricula, is to foster intentional learners who transform knowledge, rather than just retelling it. However, Bereiter claimed, students' early development of a school work module can be an obstacle for them developing into intentional learners. Our observations and interviews certainly illustrate some of the challenges that traditional beliefs about knowledge and school learning pose for the quality of students' self-regulated learning.

SUMMARY

Self-regulated learning is a deep and complex construct that encompasses a constellation of components and occurs in myriad different contexts. Not surprisingly, much about self-regulated learning remains to be understood. If we limit ourselves to any single methodological approach as we work to advance our understanding, we will be unable to capture important aspects of the whole, intricate picture. The questions that we ask and the research methods that we choose to address them function as lenses with particular focuses. Quantitative methods and surveys focus on the separate constructs of self-regulated learning, bringing the foreground into view more clearly but leaving the context less defined. Conversely, qualitative methods enable us to study the context or content of the learning, which reveals more of the panorama but blurs some of the distinctiveness of the constructs. When we try to pull those different perspectives together into a single picture, as with across-methods triangulation, we do not always find we can integrate our views perfectly and must question where the distortion and incongruities are. Measures developed in the context of traditional classroom settings may need to be revised to fit more recent forms of classroom pedagogy, such as social constructivist approaches. Grappling with the full picture in this manner is essential for us to understand, measure, and ultimately promote students' self-regulated learning better.

ACKNOWLEDGMENTS

This research was funded with support from the National Science Foundation under the following programs: REPP (REC–9720383, REC–9725927, REC–9876150), and USI (ESR–9453665). Additional funding was provided by the Spencer Foundation.

We gratefully acknowledge the support of the aforementioned agencies.

We are indebted to our collaborators in the Detroit and Chicago public schools for their ongoing partnership, and to the staff and students of the Center for Highly Interactive Computing in Education. We also thank Phyllis Blumenfeld, Graham P. Collins, and the reviewers for their helpful comments.

All opinions expressed in this work are the authors' and do not necessarily represent either the funding agencies or their universities.

REFERENCES

American Association for the Advancement of Science. (1993). *Benchmarks for science literacy*. New York: Oxford University Press.

Bereiter, C. (1990). Aspects of an educational learning theory. *Review of Educational Research, 60*, 603–624.

Blumenfeld, P. C. (1992). The task and the teacher: Enhancing student thoughtfulness in science. In J. Brophy (Ed.), *Advances in research on teaching: Planning and managing learning tasks and activities* (Vol. 3, pp. 81–114). Greenwich, CT: JAI.

Blumenfeld, P. C., Fishman, B. J., Krajcik, J. S., Marx, R. W., & Soloway, E. (2000). Creating usable innovations in systemic reform: Scaling up technology-embedded project-based science in urban schools. *Educational Psychologist, 35*, 149–164.

Blumenfeld, P. C., Marx, R. W., Patrick, H., Krajcik, J. S., & Soloway, E. (1997). Teaching for understanding. In B. J. Biddle, T. L. Good, & I. F. Goodson (Eds.), *International handbook of teachers and teaching* (Vol. II, pp. 819–878). Dordrecht, The Netherlands: Kluwer.

Blumenfeld, P. C., Soloway, E., Marx, R. W., Krajcik, J. S., Guzdial, M., & Palincsar, A. (1991). Motivating project-based learning: Sustaining the doing, supporting the learning. *Educational Psychologist, 26*, 369–398.

Brewer, J., & Hunter, A. (1989). *Multimethod research: A synthesis of styles*. Newbury Park, CA: Sage.

Denzin, N. K. (1978). *The research act: A theoretical introduction to sociological methods*. New York: McGraw-Hill.

Edelson, D. C., Gordin, D. N., & Pea, R. D. (1999). Addressing the challenges of inquiry-based learning through technology and curriculum design. *Journal of the Learning Sciences, 8*, 391–450.

Fishman, B. J., Best, S., Foster, J., & Marx, R. W. (2000, May). *Professional development in systemic reform: Using worksessions to foster change among teachers with diverse needs*. Paper presented at the meeting of the National Association of Research in Science Teaching, New Orleans, LA.

Good, T., Mulryan, C., & McCaslin, M. (1992). Grouping for instruction in mathematics: A call for programmatic research on small-group processes. In D. A. Grouws (Ed.), *Handbook of research on mathematics teaching and learning* (pp. 165–196). New York: Macmillan.

Hickey, D. T. (1997). Motivation and contemporary socio-constructivist instructional perspectives. *Educational Psychologist, 32*, 175–193.

Hofer, B. K. (2001). Personal epistemology research: Implications for learning and instruction. *Educational Psychology Review, 13*, 353–382.

Hofer, B. K., & Pintrich, P. R. (1997). The development of epistemological theories: Beliefs about knowledge and knowing and their relation to learning. *Review of Educational Research, 67*, 88–140.

Jackson, S. L., Stratford, S. J., Krajcik, J., & Soloway, E. (1994). Making dynamic modeling accessible to precollege science students. *Interactive Learning Environments, 4*, 233–257.

Krajcik, J. S., Blumenfeld, P. C., Marx, R. W., & Soloway, E. (1994). A collaborative model for helping middle grade science teachers learn project-based instruction, *Elementary School Journal, 94*, 483–497.

Lunetta, V. N. (1997). The role of laboratory in school science. In D. Tobin & B. J. Fraser (Eds.), *International handbook of science education* (pp. 249–262). Dordrecht, The Netherlands: Kluwer.

Marx, R. W., Blumenfeld, P. C., Krajcik, J. S., & Soloway, E. (1997). Enacting project-based science. *Elementary School Journal, 97*, 341–358.

McCaslin, M., & Good, T. L. (1996). *Listening in classrooms*. New York: HarperCollins.

McCaslin, M. & Hickey, D. T. (2001). Self-regulated learning and academic achievement: A Vygotskian view. In B. Zimmerman & D. Schunk (Eds.), *Self-regulated learning and academic achievement: Theoretical perspectives* (2nd ed., pp. 227–252). Mahwah, NJ: Lawrence Erlbaum Associates, Inc.

Middleton, M. J., & Blumenfeld, P. C. (2000, April). Types and sources of academic press in middle school science classrooms. In P. C. Blumenfeld (Chair), *Inquiry based science supported by technology*. Symposium conducted at the annual meeting of the American Educational Research Association, New Orleans, LA.

Midgley, C., Maehr, M. L., Hicks, L., Roeser, R., Urdan, T., Anderman, E. M., & Kaplan, A. (1996). *The patterns of adaptive learning survey (PALS)*. Ann Arbor: University of Michigan.

Miles, M. B., & Huberman, A. M. (1994). *Qualitative data analysis* (2nd ed.). Thousand Oaks, CA: Sage.

Morse, J. M. (2001). Qualitative verification: Building evidence by extending basic findings. In J. Morse, J. Swanson, & A. Kuzel (Eds.), *The nature of qualitative evidence* (pp. 203–220). Thousand Oaks, CA: Sage.

National Research Council. (1996). *National science education standards*. Washington, DC: National Academy Press.

O'Donnell, A. M., & O'Kelly, J. (1994). Learning from peers: Beyond the rhetoric of positive results. *Educational Psychology Review, 6*, 321–349.

Paris, S. G., Byrnes, J. P., & Paris, A. H. (2001). Constructing theories, identities, and actions of self-regulated learners. In B. Zimmerman & D. Schunk (Eds.), *Self-regulated learning and academic achievement: Theoretical perspectives* (2nd ed., pp. 253–287). Mahwah, NJ: Lawrence Erlbaum Associates, Inc.

Paris, S. G., & Turner, J. C. (1994). Situated motivation. In P. R. Pintrich, D. R. Brown, & C. E. Weinstein (Eds.), *Student motivation, cognition, and learning: Essays in honor of Wilbert J. McKeachie* (pp. 213–237). Hillsdale, NJ: Lawrence Erlbaum Associates, Inc.

Patrick, H., Middleton, M. J., & Taines, C. (2000, April). Urban students' motivation, collaboration, and thoughtfulness during science inquiry. In P. C. Blumenfeld (Chair), *Inquiry based science supported by technology*. Symposium conducted at the annual meeting of the American Educational Research Association, New Orleans, LA.

Pintrich, P. R., & Garcia, T. (1991). Student goal orientation and self-regulation in the college classroom. In M. L. Maehr & P. R. Pintrich (Eds.), *Advances in motivation and achievement* (Vol. 7, pp. 371–402). Greenwich, CT: JAI.

Pintrich, P. R., & Schrauben, B. (1992). Students' motivational beliefs and their cognitive engagement in classroom academic tasks. In D. Schunk & J. Meece (Eds.), *Student perceptions in the classroom* (pp. 149–183). Hillsdale, NJ: Lawrence Erlbaum Associates, Inc.

Pintrich, P. R., Smith, D. A. F., Garcia, T., & McKeachie, W. J. (1993). Reliability and predictive validity of the motivated strategies for learning questionnaire (MSLQ). *Educational and Psychological Measurement, 53*, 801–813.

Pintrich, P. R., Wolters, C. A., & Baxter, G. P. (2000). Assessing metacognition and self-regulated learning. In G. Schraw & Impara, J. C. (Eds.), *Issues in the measurement of metacognition* (pp. 43–97). Lincoln: University of Nebraska Press.

Pressley, M. (1995). More about the development of self-regulation: Complex, long-term, and thoroughly social. *Educational Psychologist, 30*, 207–212.

Putnam, R., Heaton, R., Prawat, R., & Remillard, J. (1992). Teaching mathematics for understanding: Discussing case studies of four fifth grade teachers. *Elementary School Journal, 93*, 213–228.

Richardson, V., & Anders, P. (1994). The study of teacher change. In V. Richardson (Ed.), *A theory of teacher change and the practice of staff development: A case in reading instructions* (pp. 15–180). New York: Teachers College Press.

Roth, W. M. (1995). *Authentic school science*. Dordrecht, The Netherlands: Kluwer.

Ryan, R. M., & Stiller, J. (1991). The social contexts of internalization: Parent and teacher influences on autonomy, motivation, and learning. In M. L. Maehr & P. R. Pintrich (Eds.), *Advances in motivation and achievement* (Vol. 7, pp. 115–149). Greenwich, CT: JAI.

Singer, J., Marx, R. W., Krajcik, J. S., & Chambers, J. C. (2000). Constructing extended inquiry projects: Curriculum materials for science education reform. *Educational Psychologist, 35*, 165–178.

Taines, C., Schneider, R., & Blumenfeld, P. C. (2000, April). Observations of urban middle school students engaged in technology-supported inquiry. In P. C. Blumenfeld (Chair), *Inquiry based science supported by technology*. Symposium conducted at the annual meeting of the American Educational Research Association, New Orleans, LA.

Tashakkori, A., & Teddlie, C. (1998). *Mixed methodology: Combining qualitative and quantitative approaches*. Thousand Oaks, CA: Sage.

Taylor, T. C., Fraser, B. J., & Fisher, D. L. (1997). Monitoring constructivist classroom learning environments. *International Journal of Educational Research, 27,* 293–302.

Turner, J. C., & Meyer, D. K. (1999). Integrating classroom context into motivation theory and research: Rationales, methods, and implications. In T. C. Urdan (Ed.), *Advances in motivation and achievement* (Vol. 11, pp. 87–121). Greenwich, CT: JAI.

Winne, P. H., & Perry, N. E. (2000). Measuring self-regulated learning. In M. Boekaerts, P. R. Pintrich, & M. Zeidner (Eds.), *Handbook of self-regulation: Theory, research and applications* (pp. 531–566). San Diego, CA: Academic.

Zimmerman, B. (1989). A social cognitive view of self-regulated academic learning. *Journal of Educational Psychology, 81,* 329–339.

Zimmerman, B. (1994). Dimensions of academic self-regulation: A conceptual framework for education. In D. H. Schunk & B. J. Zimmerman (Eds.), *Self-regulation of learning and performance: Issues and educational applications* (pp. 3–21). Hillsdale, NJ: Lawrence Erlbaum Associates, Inc.

EDUCATIONAL PSYCHOLOGIST, 37(1), 41–52

Learning Through Interviewing: Students and Teachers Talk About Learning and Schooling

Elisabeth Vialpando De Groot
School of Education
University of Michigan

Interviewing as an approach to studying phenomena related to self-regulated learning is the focus of this article. Three studies are presented that illustrate different interviewing approaches (unstructured, in-depth; structured; and semistructured) used to explore students' and teachers' perceptions of their experiences of learning and schooling. Examples of findings regarding components of self-regulated learning and the role of school contextual factors as facilitators and constraints on self-regulated learning are provided. Findings from these 3 studies suggest the power of interviewing for gaining a better understanding of factors related to self-regulated learning. Advantages and challenges of using each interview approach as well as future directions in research where interviewing may be a valuable approach to inquiry are discussed.

Informant: I found out that the teaching was a lot better here [new school] than over there. They dedicate more time to the student than the whole class. Like, History at the high school, I would be put at the level that the majority of the class was at for which here, I am given a pre-test and start from my level and work up which is a lot easier. … I have more control over my education and how I want to learn.

Interviewer: What makes that important?

Informant: For example, I had, it was an English class [at old high school], and I couldn't handle the work at all. It was nothing I was used to, nothing I had done before in an English class. I didn't like doing it, so I didn't do it. I didn't know how to do it, so I didn't do it. And instead of making a fool out of myself by asking questions that would seem stupid to other students and would seem like good questions to me, I'd just as soon not ask it and sit on my duff and not do nothing. I was protecting my social life and hurting my educational needs.

The purpose of this special issue is to highlight the use of qualitative techniques to enhance our understanding of self-regulated learning. Because learning through interviewing is the focus of this article, I thought it appropriate to begin with an excerpt from a lengthy interview in which a former dropout described his schooling experiences and his progress toward becoming a successful student and a more self-regulating learner. The contrast between his description of his functioning in the English class in his former high school and his perceptions of himself in his new school is striking. Elements of cognition, motivation, and goal-directed behavior emerged as critical in his self-appraisal, components that appear often in current models of self-regulated learning. Further, his description points to the importance of context as a facilitator of self-regulation. The student felt instructional practices in his new environment afforded him more opportunities to exercise choice and control, "hallmarks of self-regulation" (Schunk & Ertmer, 2000, p. 632).

To date, self-report questionnaires have been a primary method used for inquiring into issues of motivation and self-regulated learning (Brophy, 1999; Winne & Perry, 2000), and have been used frequently to investigate the relations between contextual factors and individuals' beliefs, attitudes, and behavior. Research relying on self-report data has yielded important findings. For example, studies have shown that students' motivational beliefs such as self-efficacy, task value, interest, and personal goals are related to commitment and engagement in learning including use of cognitive and self-regulating strategies (e.g., Nolen, 1988; Pajares, 1996; Pintrich & De Groot, 1990b; Pintrich & Schunk, 1996; Wolters, Yu, & Pintrich, 1996). In addition, contextual factors such as teacher support, goals for learning emphasized in school classrooms, and perceived school community have been linked to important student outcomes such as perceptions of competence, self-regulation, intrinsic motivation, task value, social and academic goals, and academic perfor-

Requests for reprints should be sent to Elisabeth Vialpando De Groot, School of Education, University of Michigan, 610 East University, Ann Arbor, MI 48109–1259. E-mail: edegroot@umich.edu

mance (e.g., Battistich, Solomon, Kim, Watson, & Schaps, 1995; De Groot, 1998; Goodenow, 1993; Midgley, Feldlaufer, & Eccles, 1989; Roeser, Midgley, & Urdan, 1996; Wentzel, 1994). However, self-report questionnaires do not permit an in-depth exploration of how individuals come to construct their own understandings within classrooms and schools or the role contextual factors play in the development of motivational beliefs and self-regulated learning. As the previous excerpt illustrates, interviewing can be a useful method for gaining a better understanding of people's experiences and the meaning of these experiences to them, and the dynamic interplay between individuals and contexts.

Through participation with colleagues in several research studies, I have had the privilege of interviewing over 200 students and teachers in a variety of different school settings. For this article, I will draw from three of these studies to illustrate different interview approaches used to gather secondary students' and teachers' perceptions of their experiences of learning and schooling. Of particular interest in this research was the role of interpersonal relationships, as well as school or classroom policies and practices, and organizational features than can facilitate or hinder student motivation, self-regulated learning, and achievement. This work was informed by social-cognitive models of self-regulated learning (e.g., Pintrich & De Groot, 1990b) and motivation (e.g., Ames, 1992a, 1992b; Anderman & Maehr, 1994; Eccles, 1983; Eccles & Midgley, 1989; Maehr & Midgley, 1996) and work from a sociological perspective on school organization and structure and social capital (e.g., Bryk, Lee, & Holland, 1993; Bryk, Lee, & Smith, 1990; Lee, Bryk, & Smith, 1993; Lee & Croninger, 1998).

In each of the first three sections of this article, brief descriptions of studies and interview approaches are provided, followed by examples of what was learned through interviews. I conclude with comments regarding some of the advantages and challenges I found when utilizing each approach, as well as speculations about future directions in educational research where interviewing might be a valuable approach to inquiry. For more detail concerning these issues, see De Groot (2002).

STUDENTS TALK ABOUT THEIR EXPERIENCES OF LEARNING IN UNSTRUCTURED, IN-DEPTH INDIVIDUAL INTERVIEWS

Purposes and Procedures

The purposes of the study were (a) to explore students' motivational beliefs and self-regulated learning, and (b) to examine intra-individual differences in beliefs and learning across different subject domains by integrating data obtained using the MSLQ (Motivated Strategies for Learning Questionnaire, see Pintrich & De Groot, 1990b), a self-report instrument with qualitative data gathered through interviews (Pintrich & De Groot, 1990a, 1993). Sixteen seventh-grade students were interviewed individually using an unstructured, in-depth interview approach. Each interview began by asking the informant to "tell me how you go about learning things for school." The students set the pace and direction of each interview with the interviewer asking clarification questions and reflecting back what was heard.

The interviews provided an opportunity to hear students as they generated rich descriptions about their own learning processes. Interviews were tape-recorded and transcribed. Transcripts were labeled by informants' initials and also by the ID number assigned to the questionnaire portion of the study to permit later comparison of the interview data with quantitative data. Transcripts were read, segments important to understanding student experience marked, and marked segments assembled into individual profiles using informant's words as much as possible. Profiles were compared to one another to look for commonalities and differences in experiences of learning (see Seidman, 1998 for expanded description).

Sample of Findings

An analysis of the qualitative data about students' experience of learning suggested that the three motivational (self-efficacy, intrinsic value, and test anxiety) and two cognitive (cognitive-strategy use and self-regulation) components tapped in the MSLQ also emerged as students talked about their own learning. However, the relations between these five components were somewhat different because of differences in the meanings students attached to these cognitive and motivational constructs.

From students' statements, it was clear that learning for these students takes place over time and has four general components: memory, strategies for information acquisition and demonstration, comprehension monitoring, and specific goals for learning. Each is necessary for learning but the process cannot be defined by any single component. One student said:

> Learning is acquiring new skills and acquiring new knowledge, something that you haven't already known. I know [when I've learned something] when I can remember most everything from what people are talking about and I know when I can think about it and tell myself everything about what I am supposed to know. I know when I know it when I can say to somebody, for instance, give them a complete answer about everything that's included in the chapter.

Students, when asked to elaborate, made particular reference to the distinction between learning and memorization. This distinction seemed to be an important assumption for students that could lead to differential use of strategies for information acquisition and different goals for their learning.

> See, if I memorize it for the test or the quiz then I forget it later. ... If you learn it, it's pretty close to remembering it years later and putting that, like applying it to something else. But if you just memorize it you might remember some of the things but that's it. Memorizing is more like to get the grades and stuff.
>
> If it makes sense to you like if you're learning a definition and you say whatever the word is and it's right but you still don't understand it, you still don't, you still wouldn't be able to use it in a sentence then you know you don't understand it. You memorized it but you don't understand it. You didn't learn it. Just because you memorize doesn't mean you understand. And learning is when you understand and memorize.

Memorization operated as a mechanism or facilitator in the service of the learning process, linked more strongly to a performance goal such as passing the test or getting the grade than a mastery goal such as understanding the subject matter. (Although this was true for the majority of the students, three students made no distinction between memorization and learning. Two students could not describe how they learned.)

The facilitator function of memorization was referred to again when students talked about the information acquisition component. When asked what happens to information so that it could be used in the learning process, one student said the following:

> Learning you can't forget as easy as you can memorizing. Once you learn something it kind of sticks in the back of your head so if you want to go back to it like if you read a book and if you're thinking about it, you'll remember it.

Students' descriptions seemed to call forth the image of the mind as "Velcro" with certain information sticking, to be translated into understanding and learning, and other information not adhering. Students also described a variety of learning strategies that helped them retain and understand information such as paraphrasing, mnemonic strategies, self-testing and self-questioning (sometimes using a tape recorder), note taking, outlining, and asking others for help. These strategies were some of the same ones asked about in the quantitative data, providing some face validity to the questionnaire we developed.

Most students seemed to be able to talk easily about what learning strategies they found particularly helpful. There was variability among students, however, with regard to the actual number of different strategies each had at their disposal to employ. It appeared that students who described themselves as better students had a greater number of strategies to choose from and used these with discretion. Those who described themselves as poorer students relied primarily on rehearsal strategies to retain and acquire information.

In addition, most students were aware that the process of learning and understanding involved both activities that observers would be able to recognize as taking place and internal activities known only to the learner. Thinking about their own thinking (metacognition) seemed to be crucial in helping them make decisions about whether they were actually comprehending information. For example, one student said, "Like when the teacher asks questions and you think to yourself if you remember the answer to that, you know it's in there [in your head]."

The learning process for the students was not confined to purely cognitive or metacognitive strategies. Motivation in terms of goals for learning was also a component. Having goals was mentioned again and again. In general, there seemed to be agreement that the goal of understanding the material (a mastery goal) was important and partially defined learning. However, students also thought getting good grades (a performance goal) played a role in learning as a kind of feedback or regulatory mechanism. For example, getting a good grade on a test in some cases was a way to validate whether the student really understood the material or not. Additionally, the knowledge that what they were studying was important to learn for future success or to meet future goals seemed to serve a self-regulatory function in terms of effort management. Here we see the close relationship between students' goals and their cognition, paralleling the strong correlations found in the quantitative data for intrinsic value, cognitive-strategy use, and self-regulation. One student's comment seemed to capture this point:

> Some people don't care if they learn or not, so maybe they don't have a motive to learn. I do because I want to get good grades and if I get good grades I want to go to U. of M. That's my motive for learning. The more I learn then the more knowledgeable I'll be and I'll get better grades. And the better grades I get, I can get into a better college and I want to go to U. of M.

This, however, was not the entire story for these students. There were other factors that students said influenced their learning, but were not essential or necessary components for learning; they either helped or hindered the process. First was intrinsic interest in the material. If material was intrinsically interesting, the interest helped them control their attention and sustain their effort even if the material was difficult. When something was perceived as "boring," students had a much harder time regulating their own learning.

> I guess like when it's interesting you wanna sort of learn a little bit more. ... It's easier for me to learn if I'm interested in it usually. Well, it's like, if the subject's interesting it's something that I want to know about. Then if they start going into something that's part of it but it's not the same thing, it's, so it gets boring because I don't

> really want to learn about it. It's hard for me to, um, keep it in there [in her head] if I'm not interested in it.
>
> It's easier to learn if it's more interesting. It's easier learning it—starting it and studying it or memorizing it. Your mind is thinking about that subject.

The second set of factors that played a role were those associated with the learning environment. Again, there appeared to be variability among students. Those who described themselves as poorer students seemed to be much more susceptible to or under the control of environmental factors such as the teacher's behavior, whether they liked the teacher, others' behavior in the classroom, and the nature of the classroom tasks. Indeed, much of their "talk" during interviews concerned classroom events and their reactions to them.

> Like maybe for a grade you'll blame her for it even though you got it [the grade], even though it was on you you'll blame her for marking it like that. Instead of you, you blame the teacher. A lot of times you feel like she's the one who marked it like that. She could have given you a break and everything or it was her fault she didn't teach it well enough.
>
> 'Cause you might be laughing about something and you'll totally miss what the teacher just said or you might be paying attention to someone else getting in trouble and you'll miss what you're supposed to be doing.

Average students did seem to be sensitive to some task demands and tried to adapt their learning accordingly. They also seemed to be somewhat more susceptible to outside influences in comparison to the better students.

> Well, I'll read the questions before I read the story. I mean, that one thing, you know, and then I'll find out what the question is and then I'll read it and then if I come across the thing that sounds like the answer then I'll write it down.
>
> Liking class has a lot to do with liking the teacher. I'll still study for it and stuff, you know, to get a good grade but it could be harder.

Better students seemed to acknowledge that environmental factors could influence learning. To what extent, however, was under their control. They seemed to be much more successful at self-regulation. For example, because they were concerned with task demands, they were more likely to spend more time and effort on school tasks and persist in the face of difficulty than other students were.

Summary Comments

Both qualitative and quantitative data suggest that motivational beliefs and cognitive and self-regulatory strategies are linked in important ways to one another in the classroom context. In addition, the interview data suggest that students may have both intrinsic, mastery goals and performance goals. Specifically, the goal of understanding material partially defined learning and getting good grades served as a feedback mechanism that can lead students to be more aware of their own strengths and weaknesses and facilitate self-regulation of learning.

What is especially noteworthy is that it was possible to hear differences between self-described better, average, and poorer students from their reflections on how they experienced their own learning. Differences were evident in three ways: how they spoke about what learning strategies or resources they used to study, their skill in regulating their effort and persistence, and how factors in their learning environment affected their own learning processes. Interestingly, when achievement data was examined later, students who described themselves as better, average, and poorer students did differ in actual achievement in terms of grades. Here is a case where interviews not only added depth and richness to the quantitative data but also provided insights into how students made connections between motivational and cognitive constructs important to their learning, and how contextual factors (e.g., teacher and peer behavior), not tapped by the questionnaire, could influence their self-regulation and learning.

STUDENTS TALK ABOUT THEIR EXPERIENCES IN A MIDDLE-LEVEL SCHOOL THAT HAD ALTERED ITS STRUCTURE IN A SERIES OF STRUCTURED INDIVIDUAL INTERVIEWS

Purposes and Procedures

A four-year collaborative study between the university and the middle school on the influence of the school environment on early adolescents was initiated because school staff was interested in monitoring student outcomes as school-reform initiatives were implemented. In response to staff concerns over the results of a school-wide (grades 7–9) student survey and recommendations from the school improvement team, the school restructured its seventh and eighth grades. The seventh grade moved to a "team" concept. Two teams of approximately 150 students and five teachers remained together for the entire year. Students traveled with the same 30 peers throughout the school day in their academic classes and gym. The changes for eighth grade were focused more on curriculum than creating a fundamentally different environment for students. Teachers were teamed but functioned more autonomously than seventh-grade teachers and there was no coordinated approach to dealing with students either academically or in terms of discipline. Students were no longer assigned to specific teams and were not with the same peers throughout the day.

The major goals of the reform were to ease the transition into junior high school; to promote a sense of community and help reduce conflicts between students and between students and staff; to promote students' investment in education; to increase students knowledge of and use of effective learning strategies to enable them to be more effective learners; and to increase students' self-esteem. In addition to these general goals, the seventh-grade structural change was accompanied by changes in educational practice: (a) the adoption of a common philosophy regarding what constituted appropriate educational experiences for early adolescents including an emphasis on collaborative learning, academic skill building, and the design of thematic units and projects to foster an understanding of the interconnectedness of disciplinary knowledge; (b) the adoption and uniform implementation of a common approach to discipline; (c) the designation of each teacher as an advisor for one group of students, which involved monitoring student attendance and academic progress as well as serving as a resource for students to go to for help; and (d) the adoption of a seventh-grade motto that stressed responsibility, reliability, and respect (the three R's) to encourage better interpersonal relationships and to help students become more successful learners.

The first class to enter the restructured school was followed from seventh-grade entry through the first semester of ninth grade. Four self-report questionnaires tapping the general areas of interest to school staff (e.g., use of learning strategies, self-regulation, motivational beliefs and goals, perceptions of and affect toward school) were administered twice each year. In addition, structured interviews were conducted with 38 students. In October of Year 1, each team of seventh-grade teachers nominated six to eight students who they believed fell into six categories: high, average, and low achievers with positive relationships with peers; and high, average, and low achievers with little or negative relations with peers. Random selection yielded 19 students per team. Students were interviewed individually three times in seventh grade, twice in eighth grade, and again in November of their ninth-grade year. Because of attrition, 35 students completed all interviews.

Interview protocols reflecting staff interests as well as those of the research team were developed and tailored for administration during each year (see Fravil & De Groot, 1995). The initial protocol contained 25 predominantly open-ended questions grouped into three areas: program–reform measures, teacher behavior, and self-appraisal–attitudes toward school. Subsequent versions contained the same areas but questions were added as students progressed through school. Peer relations and instructional–grouping practices were added as separate areas because they became more important over time. Each interview began with asking the student to "Tell me about the seventh grade (or eighth grade)," followed by "How is it different from sixth grade (or the beginning of the year)?" Other questions included "How would you describe the team program in the seventh grade?" (program–reform measures); "Can you describe what you might do in your favorite class?" (teacher behavior); "How would you describe yourself to others? What do you like most about school? Least?" (self-appraisal–attitudes toward school); "Tell me about the students in your school. What are they like in general?" (peer relations); and " Do students compete against each other for grades in your classes? Are students grouped by ability in your grade?" (instructional–grouping practices).

Interviewers were provided with the protocol and were instructed to ask questions in order unless the student had already addressed the question in another response. If a response was unclear or seemed incomplete, interviewers were told to probe for clarification (e.g., Informant: It's easier. Interviewer: How is it easier?).

Analyses of the interview data were conducted in several stages. At the end of each round of data collection, interview transcripts were sorted into the six student groups (e.g., high achiever with positive peer relations, high achiever with little or negative relations, etc.). Preliminary analyses consisted of scrutinizing responses to each question in each area. A coding scheme was developed, transcripts coded, and summaries of responses to each question were written that included the frequency that a particular item was mentioned and by whom (e.g., high achievers, girls), and sample quotes were given. From these, summaries for each area were written that also included general "tone" and interesting connections and developments. As new data were added, analyses were expanded to look for patterns and changes over time.

Sample of Findings

At the beginning of seventh grade, students reported they were adjusting to their new environment. They were still unsure about what to expect academically because the material covered had been review. Most students expressed positive feelings about school, their teachers, and peers. For example, all Team B students mentioned they liked Mr. C. He made them think, didn't use worksheets, and helped them see how what they were learning was related to their lives beyond school. Although few could describe the team program or its goals, some recognized that teachers worked together and talked with one another about students, there was a uniform discipline policy, and the three "Rs" (respectful, responsible, reliable) were stressed.

> [The program] It's not trying to make you fail, it's just trying to help you succeed. In your grades and stuff. Like if you get a bad grade on a test, they ain't gonna make you fail. They let you take it over to get a better grade and succeed in grades.
>
> [About teams] I don't know. I just heard some of the teachers talking about how it, how they say it's supposed to help because they all get together and talk

about the same problems that one person or student has and then they just talk about the whole thing.

[About encouragement] I don't know, they're always saying I *can* do it. I just don't wanna do it. They say I rush through all my work and—they always try to help.

By mid-year, students viewed the program as helpful and most felt they were doing better academically because of the amount of support they received from teachers and peers. In terms of policies and instructional practices, students gave several reasons for the use of collaborative learning and the discipline code. This may be because teachers discussed reasons for both with students on a regular basis. Many students commented on the importance of being able to work cooperatively in the classroom as preparation for their future work lives. As noted in the first study, the idea that what students were doing in school was useful and relevant to their future encouraged effort and engagement in learning. Other students noted the help peers provided in understanding concepts and completing difficult assignments. As far as the discipline code was concerned, students saw it as fair and felt it was applied fairly to all students, which helped create a positive atmosphere.

By the end of seventh grade, student responses were more variable. When asked about differences between the beginning and ending of the school year, some students felt there were few differences. However, many felt things had changed:

The teachers are, like, they try to get more out of you to get it right and stuff.

It's a lot harder now than at the beginning of the year because they wanted to get you off to a good start. And the more harder the work gets, the more bad grades I get—because it teaches me more. I think I'm getting more out of it now.

Teachers have gotten a lot stricter. ... When we came from sixth grade, they just wanted to start us off on a slow process. But now we're getting really into the curriculum that's a lot more fast-paced. But we're used to it. It's really getting harder but we're used to it.

It is interesting to note that many students felt they were learning more toward the end of the year. However, it seemed that what students were commenting on was that more new material was being presented to them to learn; not that they were actually mastering the content. Still, most students felt efficacious, even those not doing well. In addition, many students felt teachers were more demanding. Although effort was still stressed, the emphasis seemed to have shifted from making progress to "getting it right."

Moreover, differential treatment of students was becoming noticeable. High-achieving students received more opportunities for interactions with teachers, group work, and special projects. Some low-achieving students felt they were not treated as well as high-achieving students by teachers and some peers. Further, students seemed to be slightly more negative about school than earlier in the year.

Students also talked extensively about the assignment notebooks. To assist students in developing appropriate study strategies and monitoring their own progress and behavior, each student had been given an assignment planner. As one student described it,

We have to, like, write down what we did in that class and like on that date. We wrote like what we did and what we have to finish. ... They're good. They helped me out. Like, I would look back like after seventh hour and see like what homework I have and like take what I had to do [home with me]. I'd probably still be organized, but not as much as I am.

Students were required to have the assignment notebooks signed by parents every week. On Mondays, teachers checked for signatures and made sure students had filled the information in properly. Some students, especially average achievers, believed the planners helped them to monitor and regulate their own behavior. However, high achievers seemed to believe they were self-regulating already and did not need teachers to monitor their behavior.

In terms of the team program, all students listed a number of benefits. Average and lower achieving students were particularly complimentary, whereas most of the high-achieving students felt they would not have needed the team structure to assist them in the transition because they were sufficiently mature, organized, and academically capable to adapt well on their own. The majority of the students felt the program was beneficial to incoming seventh graders and wanted to see it continued for this group. It allowed students to adjust more easily to a bigger school with many more people and a number of different teachers. However, only about 25% wanted the teams continued into eighth grade. The main reason for discontinuation was social—they wanted to meet more students.

In initial eighth-grade interviews, students did not recognize that a modified team structure even existed. Although they thought teachers were supposed to be working together, they saw no evidence that this was happening. More students saw the benefits of the team program now. In particular, they missed how the teachers worked together in providing support for students and in coordinating instruction and homework demands. Students complained about the lack of consistency in discipline and in grading practices and did not like the lecture format used in most classes. They also said that teachers called attention to grades often and treated those students who got good grades better than those who did not do as well. In general, students were very negative about teachers and school. Many felt they were not performing as well academically as they could be or should be because of the differences in instructional practices. Students also talked about how things like the three "Rs" made a difference in the classroom atmosphere and in their motivation. In general, the high-achieving students were the ones who continued to be the most motivated in their studies and positive about school.

Interestingly, many students thought the seventh grade had been "harder" in some ways than the eighth grade. Students thought their seventh-grade teachers had had higher expectations, had been tougher overall, and grades had been lower (analysis of grades supported students' remarks). However, teachers had been more responsive to student questions in class, provided more help, and had students frequently work in groups so they could help one another. Eighth grade was harder than seventh grade because teachers were less approachable, were more demanding in terms of homework, and material was being presented at a faster rate through lecture. As one student said, "Once you get into higher grades, teachers get harder. Lectures, notes, and more homework. Lectures, notes, and tests. That's all we do." By the end of eighth grade, students were negative about school and nostalgic about the team program. What they liked was that they got to meet more students. When asked about their expectations for ninth grade, students believed it would be the same as eighth grade.

Summary Comments

Although it was not possible to do more than touch on what can be gained when using this approach to interviewing, what was presented served as an illustration. First, students perceived changes in the school–classroom environment over time. There was a decline in opportunities for group work, the amount of content covered increased whereas the amount of explanation and discussion of content decreased, instruction became more teacher-led and less student-centered, and there was increased variability among teachers in terms of grading practices and discipline. In addition, it appeared that classroom goal structure became more ability focused and less task focused, teacher support in terms of helping, caring, and listening to students declined, and students reported an increase in differential treatment of higher and lower ability students. Most of these represent differences students noted between the seventh and eighth grade.

Second, as these changes occurred, most students became increasingly negative about school. Further, students seemed to become more performance-oriented. For example, when asked what frustrates them in school, responses moved from "nothing" or feelings of frustration when they wanted to understand something but were having difficulties to frustration over not getting better grades. When asked about whether students competed against each other for grades, the responses shifted from "No" accompanied by puzzled looks to answers such as, "They fight about who gets the best grades, who made the honor roll."

Third, students also identified reform practices and teacher behaviors that facilitated their motivation and self-regulation. The emphasis on responsible, reliable, and respectful behavior and attitudes in the classroom and the assignment planners helped some students become more self-monitoring and better able to regulate their own learning behaviors. Teachers' use of collaborative learning and their explanations of how what students were doing and learning in school was important to their future made a difference in students' effort and persistence on tasks and active engagement in learning. Additionally, teachers' working together and their responsiveness to student needs helped students feel more cared about and more confident that they could master material through their own efforts.

In this study, both self-report questionnaires and interviews were used to complement one another to yield a better picture of how students experienced the school environment, how they perceived themselves over time, and the relations between the two. Although self-report questionnaires could provide data on some areas of concern to school personnel (e.g., use of learning strategies, motivational beliefs, feelings and perceptions about school and schoolwork), structured interviews yielded critical information that helped make the quantitative data more meaningful and also provided insights into areas (e.g., teacher–student relations, reform measures) and changes over time in students' experiences that our questionnaires could not tap.

STUDENTS AND TEACHERS TALK ABOUT THE SCHOOL AS "COMMUNITY" IN SEMISTRUCTURED FOCUS GROUP INTERVIEWS

Purposes and Procedures

Recently, I had the opportunity to work with Valerie Lee and Robert Croninger, sociologists of education, on their research project: "Social Capital and Its Effects on the Academic Development of Adolescents At Risk for Educational Failure." Although both researchers are known for their quantitative work, only qualitative methods were employed in this study. The purposes of the study were to examine (a) how social capital is generated and sustained in high schools, and (b) how social capital in schools promotes the academic and social development of students at-risk for educational failure. The school was the unit of analysis. To address study questions, six schools were explored in-depth using multiple inquiry approaches, and case studies were written for each school.

I will focus on one school, St. X. (pseudonym), a small Catholic high school, in which I functioned as Lead Researcher. Primary data collection occurred during two one-week visitations, one in the fall and one in spring of a single school year. Semistructured focus group interviews were conducted with students, teachers, and parents. Numbers in these groups varied from three to ten. Interview guides with open-ended questions tapping specific areas of interest to researchers were used. Each began with an introductory script reviewing the nature of study. A general question followed by more specific questions was provided in each guide. However, these guides were to function more as a tool for interviewers to help focus the discussion than as a set of questions to be asked in a specific order. Interviewers were to follow the lead of their informants, working the areas of interest into the conversation. Questions focused on five areas for student focus groups: beliefs about the school's mission, the school's social environment, the kinds of problems students have in school, the assistance provided to students to resolve problems, and students' perceptions of teachers. The first four areas were the same for teacher interviews, whereas the fifth area inquired into teachers' perceptions of teacher–parent and school–community relations. In addition, some teachers and other members of the school staff were interviewed individually using semistructured and unstructured approaches. Occasionally, staff members were interviewed more than once to help clarify perspectives and perceptions.

Interviews were tape-recorded and transcribed. Transcripts were read and segments labeled using categories derived from the conceptual framework and accompanying research questions (e.g., school mission, teacher–student relationships). Coded excerpts were put into files (sometimes into more than one file), then each file was examined and sometimes subdivided into smaller units and recoded to reflect the change. In the final steps, themes were constructed from connections that emerged between categories.

Sample of Findings

It is impossible to do more than touch on some of what our informants shared with us about their perceptions of their school experiences. Because of its relation to the issue of the role of context in motivation and self-regulated learning, I will share what emerged as a central theme in our inquiry: the "sense of community" in this school.

Teachers talk about their school.

> They just kinds, they become a whole person here. They develop a confidence and a broad perspective. They're better prepared for college and for the world because of the sense of relationship they had here.
>
> What I realized was, because I had not spent much time in other schools, is how engaged our students and our faculty are. So engaged. The engagement, the interaction, the relationships. Here, there's always a give and take, whether it be in the hall and in the school, constantly, you'll see teachers in the hall talking to kids and vise versa, always. About all kinds of things. There's this whole thing going on. It states that there really is a sense of place about this program.

As these quotes suggest, teachers believed "There's this whole thing going on" that set this school apart from others. The majority of the adults in this school had made a commitment to a common vision, to creating an environment described in words such as family atmosphere, sense of place, stability, support, strict, accepting, and caring. Indeed, as one teacher articulated, many teachers who chose to remain despite more lucrative prospects elsewhere did so because they felt a sense of purpose. Another teacher followed up on his colleague's comment by saying, "Talk with those who have left for the public schools, for the higher salaries or what have you. Almost without exception, they'll say, 'Ya, salary's great; but I miss the community. I miss the kids.'" The word "community" was used again and again and it took us a while to realize that what people were talking about was the school as "community," a sense of belonging, not a geographic locale. This school had a clearly stated mission and goals that the staff worked hard to carry out. Further, a particular route had been chosen to accomplish their purpose and new faculty and students were socialized accordingly.

Teachers communicated high expectations for academic performance and appropriate behavior to students, but actively helped students meet these expectations. They stated they tried to impress on students that everything they did in school including participation in extracurricular activities was important to their growth and development. Further, teachers modeled what they expected from students in their own behavior. Many teachers sponsored clubs themselves or attended after-school events on a regular basis. They also spoke of the support and help they gave and received from other teachers and administrators.

Students talk about their school.

> Interviewer: Just to start with, what I'd like to know from you is how you'd characterize this school in terms of support, the kind of support that students get. ...
>
> Informant 1: I think that the school is very supportive because there are so many people that you can talk to. If you get to one of your teachers, there's guidance counselors you can talk to, security guards, you can talk to, anyone. I mean, if they're there, then it feels comfortable around the faculty at St. X.
>
> Informant 2: Well, I think that the school is highly supportive too. I've been through a lot so far as school-wise and needing help and stuff and I know I pulled out of it because of all the support that I've had from my counselor and from my teachers. Responding to me and stuff. So, I think it's highly supportive.
>
> Interviewer: OK.
>
> Informant 3: I think it's supportive because I've been through a lot home-wise and I've had teachers help me through things with my school and, plus, with problems I have at home. They've been there for me.

In focus group interviews, students were very willing to express their opinions on the school in general and to share their personal experiences openly with peers. Indeed, one of the challenges was to manage the time so that all students who wanted to could give their perspective. Most students felt that the school helped prepare them academically, that there were supports available to them for academic and personal difficulties, that most teachers held high expectations for students, and that they received encouragement to do their best. They also spoke of the opportunities provided to become involved in activities that matched their interests and the recognition that there was a basic set of rules by which everyone abided, including teachers.

In contrast to what we heard from faculty, students seemed to believe there was some variability among teachers in terms of who could be relied on for support, what form that support might take, and equal treatment of all students. Some teachers were seen as providing only academic help to students, others who could be consulted about any problem, and still others who were perceived as unapproachable. In addition, students believed that some teachers had "favorites" and the favored students were given more latitude in terms of their behavior in class. What was remarkable, however, was that students noticed variations in these areas among teachers, expressed their feelings about them, but didn't seem to focus on these as things that interfered with the overall sense of "community" most felt was present in this school.

The sense of community arose again when students spoke about their relationships with peers:

> Unity. Like everybody's so, it's like a whole big family here. If one person has a problem, everybody has a problem.
>
> OK, I don't talk to some of these people everyday, but this is like my family, kind of. I might not get along with all of them, but we still, I just don't know how I would graduate without them or whatever.

They felt peers got along well with one another and that there were few students in the school who did not seem to fit in socially. Although there was some suggestion that freshman year was particularly difficult because students had not learned the norms regarding appropriate behavior yet, only a few students continued to have problems being accepted. As in any family, however, conflicts did occur. Most reported that conflicts were not a group phenomenon but occurred more often between individuals. Unlike teacher reports, however, students did indicate that small fights or "skirmishes" happened regularly among both males and females. These arguments seldom escalated into large fights mainly because students intervened with their peers to calm the situation.

Further, students helped one another academically. Indeed, they believed the help and support they received from peers was as important to their academic success as that provided by teachers. Peers tutored one another and felt free to ask for help when needed. At the same time, the majority of students reported that intense competition for grades went on in this school.

> Informant: Well, for me mostly, like me and my friends, in school and out of school, we always comparing grades. Like some people out of school and even some people in school, they, like, some people seem kind of proud to be doing bad in school. But other people, I don't know why, we are always comparing saying, ah, I got better than you second quarter. You stupid. We just playing around and stuff and so we always like compete with each other and get our better grades than each other. But, we mostly support each other like that.
>
> Interviewer: Is it OK to be smart in this school?
>
> Informant: Ya, I think that's good because if you, report cards come out, it's like a competition with just about downright everybody. Who's going to make the honor roll? Everybody's running to the board and saying, 'What's your GPA?' They're like, 3.6, they're like, ha, 3.714. I'm saying the numbers just roll right off their tongue and they'll see it one time and they'll, 4.372. And they just come right out with it and it's like everybody's trying to be better than their friend and their friend's got 3.7 and they're trying to get 3.8.
>
> Interviewer: What if somebody doesn't do well?
>
> Informant: You encourage them. Ya, that's what I like about this school. Because if you do something good, it's not just one person will congratulate you. The whole school will be behind you. They'll be like, 'Ya, you did good, good job, good job.' But if you did bad, they ain't gonna put you down or nothing. They'll just, everyone will be like, oh, you can do better, you will do better. I'll help you.

There was a great deal of comparison of grades and a heightened awareness of where students ranked relative to their peers. As one student said of another, "Everybody knows she sits on top."

It is interesting to note that the majority of students said that the competition and social comparison that went on did not have a negative impact in this environment. Rather, it provided them with an incentive to want to do better and did not interfere with their relationships with one another. Indeed, even students who admitted they didn't do well felt supported by their peers, especially when they became discouraged. No one was going to go out of his or her way to put someone down, only try to help. Given the current debate among motivation researchers coming from a goal theory perspective regarding the operation of mastery and performance goals (e.g., Midgley, Kaplan, & Middleton, 2001), these student descriptions are particularly provocative.

It was clear that teachers and students had different perceptions of what went on in this school. However, there seemed to be general agreement that a sense of "community" was fostered. Within this context of community, there appeared to be active participation and investment in school among the majority of the faculty and students.

Summary Comments

As one can see, the use of the semistructured interview approach with focus groups allowed us access to students' and teachers' perceptions of this school, particularly the nature of social relationships between school members, beliefs regarding the school's mission, and what was expected of individuals in this school. As individuals talked about their experiences, we were able to hear the importance and impact of a powerful school culture on teacher efficacy and morale, and student effort on school tasks, valuing of school, self-efficacy, and goals for learning. The data from this study suggest that school culture plays an important role in students' academic development and needs to be considered when trying to understand how motivational beliefs and self-regulatory skills develop in school.

COMMENTS CONCERNING INTERVIEW APPROACHES

In this article I provided examples of different interview approaches and how interviewing could provide valuable information regarding motivation and self-regulated learning, and the role of context. Briefly, I would like to comment on what I believe to be some practical considerations regarding the use of the different interview approaches. This is not intended to be a comprehensive examination, merely a look at some of the advantages and challenges I found when utilizing each approach. There are many excellent sources available that explore the different approaches and their utilization, as well as data analysis in depth (e.g., LeCompte & Schensul, 1999; Miles & Huberman, 1994; Schensul, Schensul, & LeCompte, 1999; Schensul, LeCompte, Nastasi, & Borgatti, 1999; Seidman, 1998; Weiss, 1994).

Unstructured, In-Depth Interviews

In the first study, individual unstructured, in-depth interviews were conducted to explore students' perceptions of how they learned things for school. The interview and questionnaire components of the study were treated as separate "studies" and later combined to yield what was presented here. In planning the interview component, I was interested in how students made meaning of their experiences, what they believed to be important to their learning, not in finding support for constructs tapped in the questionnaire or gaining answers to specific questions. The unstructured approach allowed students to tell their own stories in their own way, yielding rich descriptions of themselves and their experiences that, in my opinion, could not have been obtained in any other way.

However, conducting these interviews was no easy task and required a significant investment in terms of time and effort. It was critical that informants had enough time to talk until they believed they were finished. This was especially challenging because we were interviewing students during the school day and considerable negotiation with school staff ahead of time was necessary. In addition, utilizing this approach effectively requires that interviewers have considerable skills in in-depth interviewing techniques so they can facilitate rather than direct and seek to uncover informants' perspectives, not assume shared understandings. The quality of the data depends exclusively on the skill of the interviewer. Although the two of us who were conducting interviews had considerable experience, we each conducted a practice interview and then worked together for several hours studying the transcripts and practicing our skills before entering the field. If more than one interviewer is used regardless of the interview approach taken, I believe it critical that adequate time is allocated for training and practice.

Structured Interviews

In contrast to the first study, the second study used a structured approach. A series of six individual interviews were conducted over 2½ years. There were several advantages to using this approach in this case. We found it was possible to gather student perspectives on a variety of areas of interest in a relatively short period of time. In addition, although this approach still required interviewers to possess some skills, these could be developed in less time as part of the training in the use of the interview instrument. Because training took less time, we could add interviewers during the course of the study. Further, we found that having an interview protocol was very helpful when it came to data analysis. Preliminary analyses could be done in a relatively short period of time and the findings speedily reported to our collaborators in the school who needed them to make school improvement decisions.

Although there were advantages to this approach, challenges also were identified. First was the development of the instrument itself. We found it very difficult to craft a protocol where the questions built on one another so that there would be a flow to the actual interview. This was my first attempt at protocol design and it showed. Transcripts from the practice interviews read like disjointed verbal questionnaires and students' responses reflected the abrupt shifts in thinking that were needed to respond to questions as they were asked. In some sense, the nature of this approach makes this unavoidable. Although adjustments were made and useful information was gained from the interviews, this experience clearly demonstrates the need to devote significant time and attention to instrument development.

Second, by its very nature, the structured approach is limiting. We designed the interview portion of the study to supplement the quantitative piece. Although this format served our research needs, we were aware in our planning that we were making choices to explore some areas and not others. However, some significant issues emerged during the first years' round of interviews that we had not considered initially. Consequently, the protocol was altered for the next rounds to allow us to explore these areas. Because of the longitudinal nature of the study, we were able to do this. However, it made us very aware of what can be missed when using this interviewing approach.

Semistructured Interviews

In the third study, semistructured focus group interviews with students and teachers were conducted. Interview guides with open-ended questions were developed. This approach was chosen for this study to insure a degree of comparability across sites and yet allow for sensitivity to each school's uniqueness (Miles & Huberman, 1994). As the name implies, this approach combines some of the advantages of both the unstructured and structured formats discussed previously. It also shares some of the drawbacks.

Of particular concern for this study was the use of multiple interviewers in multiple sites. Although the interview guides used were consistent across sites, researchers were not. A different team assumed responsibility for each school. In addition, not all researchers who were part of a team in a given school were from the same university. Although these may seem like small matters, we found they could present a significant challenge in terms of trying to conduct any extensive training before entering the field. This approach requires a good deal of skill on the part of the interviewer, especially when conducting focus group interviews. Interviewers need to be able to attend to many individuals at the same time, as well as providing some direction to the discussion while still allowing informants to convey what they believe to be critical to their experiences in the school setting. Pairing an experienced interviewer with a less experienced one, as we did for this study, can be very helpful. However, providing training and practice is always the preferable option.

The second concern involves choosing to conduct focus groups rather than individual interviews. Because we were interested in gathering as much information as possible in a short period of time about individuals' perceptions and how individuals interacted with one another, the focus group was a good choice. However, we became aware of some limitations of group interviews. First, the larger the group, the more difficult it was to gather multiple perspectives on the range of areas we thought important to investigate and still keep interview times reasonable. I included an excerpt from a 10-member student focus group in the last section to illustrate this point. Second, in our small school (approximately 700 students and 63 full- and part-time teachers), we became concerned that teachers in particular were reluctant to express divergent opinions in a highly public forum such as a focus group. After all, they will continue to live in this environment long after researchers have left. Although we had the opportunity to enhance our understanding of individuals' perspectives by conducting individual interviews, I think these are important considerations.

FUTURE DIRECTIONS

The turn of the century and the beginning of a new millennium have prompted many reflections on past practices and future directions. In an article on educational research for the 21st century, Schoenfeld (1999) urged researchers to locate their work in Pasteur's quadrant, use-inspired basic research.[1] He noted that

> Educational research has evolved to the point where it is possible, much of the time, to conduct research in contexts that are of practical import, working on problems whose solutions help make things better and contribute to theoretical understanding. Finding and working on such problems is a high-leverage strategy for making a difference in the years to come. (p. 5)

In his discussion of theoretical issues (e.g., theories of learning) and issues of practice (e.g., how changes in the learning environment affect student outcomes) that require further attention, Schoenfeld suggested the need to transcend disciplinary boundaries, to integrate diverse theoretical perspectives, and to devise and adopt new approaches to inquiry.

It is interesting to note that Pintrich (2000) made some of the same points in his final editorial for *Educational Psychologist.* He outlined four themes that emerged in his review of articles published in this journal over the past 5 years, themes that would likely continue as foci of research in the future: (a) a multidimensional view of the individual learner; (b) concern with an expanded range of outcomes of schooling; (c) using nontraditional models and constructs to understand learning and development; and (d) understanding the individual in context. In his discussion, he speculated that the fourth theme would dominate future research. Further, like Schoenfeld, Pintrich suggested that "much of educational psychological research in the future should fit into Pasteur's quadrant" (p.224).

In contemplating these future directions for research, I suggest that interviewing, like other techniques outlined in this special issue, will continue to be a very useful qualitative approach to inquiry into complex educational phenomena. Throughout this article, I tried to stress the power of this approach for gaining a better understanding of how motivational and cognitive components of self-regulated learning

---

[1]See Stokes's (1997) reconceptualization of the basic-applied continuum view of research goals into a four-cell matrix with fundamental understanding and usefulness or utility representing separate dimensions. Because of Pasteur's concern with both microbiological mechanisms of disease and spoilage prevention, Stokes labeled the use-inspired basic research quadrant in his design as Pasteur' quadrant.

interact to produce learning and development. This will help us achieve a more multidimensional view of the learner and add to our theoretical understanding of self-regulation processes. At the same time, as has been noted repeatedly throughout this article, interviewing methodology highlights the importance of considering the role of context in motivation and self-regulation. In this manner, interviewing methodology contributes not only to our theoretical understanding of self-regulation processes, but also to our understanding of the development of the individual in context, an important goal for educational psychology.

REFERENCES

Ames, C. (1992a). Achievement goals and the classroom motivational climate. In D. Schunk & J. Meece (Eds.), *Student perceptions in the classroom: Causes and consequences* (pp. 327–348). Hillsdale, NJ: Lawrence Erlbaum Associates, Inc.

Ames, C. (1992b). Classrooms: Goals, structures, and student motivation. *Journal of Educational Psychology, 84,* 261–271.

Anderman, E., & Maehr, M. L. (1994). Motivation and schooling in the middle grades. *Review of Educational Research, 64,* 287–309.

Battistich, V., Solomon, D., Kim, D., Watson, M., & Schaps, E. (1995). Schools as communities, poverty levels of student populations, and students' attitudes, motives, and performance: A multilevel analysis. *American Education Research Journal, 32*(3), 627–658.

Brophy, J. (1999). Research on motivation in education: Past, present, and future. In M. L. Maehr, P. R. Pintrich, & T. C. Urdan (Eds.), *Advances in motivation and achievement: The role of context* (Vol. 11, pp. 1–44). Stamford, CT: JAI.

Bryk, A. S., Lee, V. E., & Holland, P. B. (1993). *Catholic schools and the common good.* Cambridge, MA: Harvard University Press.

Bryk, A. S., Lee, V. E., & Smith, J. B. (1990). High school organization and its effects on teachers and students: An interpretive summary of the research. In W. T. Cline & J. F. Witte (Eds.), *Choice and control in American education* (Vol. 1, pp. 135–226). Philadelphia: Falmer.

De Groot, E. V. (2002). In their own words: Students and teachers talk about learning and schooling. In M. L. Maehr & P. R. Pintrich (Eds.), *Advances in motivation and achievement* (Vol. 12, pp. 157–206. Oxford, England, JAI.

Eccles, J. (1983) Expectancies, values, and achievement behaviors. In J. T. Spence (Ed.), *Achievement and achievement motives* (pp. 75–146). San Francisco: Freeman.

Eccles, J., & Midgley, C. (1989). Stage-environment fit: Developmentally appropriate classrooms for young adolescents. In C. Ames & R. Ames (Eds.), *Research on motivation in education* (Vol. 3, pp. 139–186). San Diego, CA: Academic.

Fravil, K., & De Groot, E. V. (1995, April). *Early adolescents' perceptions of school reform.* Paper presented at the annual meeting of the American Educational Research Association, San Francisco, CA.

Goodenow, C. (1993). Classroom belonging among early adolescent students: Relationship to motivation and achievement. *Journal of Early Adolescence, 13,* 12–43.

LeCompte, M. D., & Schensul, J. J. (1999). *Designing and conducting ethnographic research.* Walnut Creek, CA: AltaMira Press.

Lee, V. E., Bryk, A. S., & Smith, J. B. (1993). The organization of effective high schools. In L. Darling-Hammond (Ed.), *Review of Research in Education* (Vol. 19, pp. 171–267). Washington, DC: American Educational Research Association.

Lee, V. E., & Croninger, R. G. (1998, April). *Elements of social capital in the context of six high schools.* Paper presented at "Social Capital: An International Conference Bridging Disciplines, Policies, and Communities." East Lansing: Michigan State University.

Maehr, M. L., & Midgley, C. (1996). *Transforming school cultures.* Boulder, CO: Westview.

Midgley, C., Feldlaufer, H., & Eccles, J. S. (1989). Student/teacher relations and attitudes toward mathematics before and after the transition to junior high school. *Child Development, 60,* 981–992.

Midgley, C., Kaplan, A., & Middleton, M. (2001). Performance approach goals: Good for what, for whom, under what circumstances, and at what cost? *Journal of Educational Psychology, 93,* 77–86.

Miles, M. B., & Huberman, M. (1994). *Qualitative data analysis.* Thousand Oaks, CA: Sage.

Nolen, S. (1988). Reasons for studying: Motivational orientations and study strategies. *Cognition and Instruction, 5,* 269–287.

Pajares, F. (1996). Self-efficacy beliefs in academic settings. *Review of Educational Research, 66,* 543–578.

Pintrich, P. R. (2000). Educational psychology at the millennium: A look back and a look forward. *Educational Psychologist, 35*(4), 221–226.

Pintrich, P. R., & De Groot, E. V. (1993, April). *Narrative and paradigmatic perspectives on measuring student motivation and self-regulated learning in the classroom context.* Paper presented at the annual meeting of the American Educational Research Association, Atlanta, GA.

Pintrich, P. R., & De Groot, E. V. (1990a, April). *Quantitative and qualitative perspectives on student motivational beliefs and self-regulated learning.* Paper presented at the annual meeting of the American Educational Research Association, Boston, MA.

Pintrich, P. R., & De Groot, E. V. (1990b). Motivational and self-regulated learning components of classroom academic performance. *Journal of Educational Psychology, 82,* 33–40.

Pintrich, P. R., & Schunk, D. H. (1996). *Motivation in education: Theory, research and applications.* Englewood Cliffs, NJ: Merrill Prentice-Hall.

Roeser, R., Midgley, C., & Urdan, T. (1996). Perceptions of the school psychological environment and early adolescents' psychological and behavioral functioning in school: The mediating role of goals and belonging. *Journal of Educational Psychology, 88,* 408–422.

Schensul, J. J., LeCompte, M. D., Nastasi, B. K., & Borgatti, S. P. (1999). *Enhanced ethnographic methods.* Walnut Creek, CA: AltaMira Press.

Schensul, S. L., Schensul, J. J., & LeCompte, M. D. (1999). *Essential ethnographic methods.* Walnut Creek, CA: AltaMira Press.

Schoenfeld, A. H. (1999). Looking toward the 21st century: Challenges of educational theory and practice. *Educational Researcher, 28*(7), 4–14.

Schunk, D. H., & Ertmer, P. A. (2000). Self-regulation of academic learning: Self-efficacy enhancing interventions. In M. Boekaerts, P. R. Pintrich, & M. Zeidner (Eds.), *Handbook of self-regulation* (pp. 631–649). San Diego, CA: Academic.

Seidman, I. (1998). *Interviewing as qualitative research: A guide for researchers in education and the social sciences.* New York: Teachers College Press.

Stokes, D. E. (1997). *Pasteur's quadrant: Basic science and technical innovation.* Washington, DC: Brookings Institute.

Weiss, R. S. (1994). *Learning from strangers: The art and method of qualitative interview studies.* New York: Free Press.

Wentzel, K. R. (1994). The relations of social goal pursuit to social acceptance, classroom behavior and perceived social support. *Journal of Educational Psychology, 86,* 173–182.

Winne, P. H., & Perry, N. E. (2000). Measuring self-regulated learning. In M. Boekaerts, P. R. Pintrich, & M. Zeidner (Eds.), *Handbook of self-regulation* (pp. 532–566). San Diego, CA: Academic.

Wolters, C., Yu, S., & Pintrich, P. R. (1996). The relation between goal orientation and students' motivational beliefs and self-regulated learning. *Learning and Individual Differences, 8,* 211–232.

EDUCATIONAL PSYCHOLOGIST, *37*(1), 53–57

Investigating the Interface Between Self-Regulation and Involvement Processes

JoyLynn H. Reed
School of Arts and Humanities
University of Texas at Dallas

Diane L. Schallert and Leta F. Deithloff
Department of Educational Psychology
University of Texas at Austin

This article considers how the processes that lead to involvement, defined as psychological engrossment, could be construed as mutually exclusive of what is meant by self-regulation, a metacognitive process that requires strategic and motivational control. However, this article proposes that much can be learned by attempting to capture the phase change in a task when self-regulatory processes disappear and a new, nonself-focused state takes over. The contribution to the self-regulation literature arises from an open-ended qualitative approach focused on the distinct phases of a task to reveal the role self-regulation can play in concert with other processes. This article elaborates on the ways self-regulation is connected to the nonregulative process of involvement.

At first glance, the process of involvement, defined as the attentional operations that lead to psychological engrossment, could be construed as mutually exclusive of the metacognitive processes required for self-regulation. With its strong focus on strategies and motivational control (Zimmerman, 1990), self-regulation would seem antithetical with the sort of "flow" experience described by Csikszentmihalyi (1990) that we have come to identify with involvement. Those characteristics of deep involvement that include being totally immersed in a task with little self-consciousness would seem to imply that self-regulation and involvement are incompatible. However, our many investigations have pointed to how self-regulation may in fact be tied to involvement as an antecedent to the process, a stimulus that uses volitional strategies to move a learner from a self-focused state into immersion in a task (cf. Reed, Hagen, Wicker, & Schallert, 1996; Reed & Schallert, 1993; Schallert & Reed, 1997). Similarly, we contend that progress can be made in understanding the mechanisms of self-regulation by looking at its junction with a nonregulatory process such as involvement. In the first section, we describe our work on involvement, distinguishing it from the related constructs of interest and engagement. Next, we discuss some of the more important methodological issues we see surrounding the study of involvement. Third, we address the relationship between involvement and self-regulation. Fourth, we elaborate on how we can understand a task better by studying its component phases. We conclude by discussing what can be learned about self-regulation from a qualitative look at its interface with involvement.

Requests for reprints should be sent to JoyLynn H. Reed, Department of Educational Psychology, University of Texas at Dallas, P.O. Box 830688, Mail Stop JO31, Richardson, TX 75083. E-mail: jhr@onr.com

THE CONSTRUCT OF INVOLVEMENT

When we began our study of involvement, we had not yet connected our description of the process either to Csikszentmihalyi's concept of flow or to the related constructs of interest and engagement. Instead, the impetus for our work was Deborah Tannen's (1985) notion of discourse involvement and our hope to extend its description of conversational processes to students' participation in academic discourse tasks.

Issues of Definition

Here it may be useful to provide a fuller description of what we mean by involvement by distinguishing it from related constructs often used interchangeably with the term, interest and engagement. Engagement is more general than involvement in terms of what it encompasses. Representative are the views of Guthrie, Van Meter, and their colleagues (1996), who described engagement as "the integration of motivations and strategies in literacy activities" (p. 306) and further explained that "both intrinsic and extrinsic motivational states are included in the definition of engagement and engagement refers to a set of activity-related processes rather than a psychological state" (p. 306). Most of the research on engagement has focused on students' participation in classroom activities.

A common belief is that involvement is the same thing as interest. Although we recognize that the literature on interest is vast with its own intriguing competing theories, we focus here on Krapp, Hidi, and Renninger's (1992) view because it has been most influential in educational psychology in the past 10 years. Interest, as they described it, can either be individual "dispositions that develop over time" (p. 6) or situational and "generated by certain stimulus characteristics (e.g., life themes, novelty) that tend to be shared among individuals" (p. 6). Although not a strategic processing variable, interest is more of either a trigger to attention or an aid to memory, or both, leading to engagement and perhaps involvement.

Involvement is a psychological process described as follows: "When an individual is involved in a task, his or her attention is wholly concentrated on that task, making a sense of time irrelevant and coinciding with deep comprehension of the task material" (Reed et al., 1996). As we define it, involvement is a special type of engagement (cf. Guthrie & Wigfield, 1997; Schallert & Reed, 1997). Engagement subsumes involvement because it is not possible to be involved without being engaged; however, it is possible to be engaged without being involved. Further, involvement is related to interest in that being interested may be an antecedent, and even converted into a volitional strategy for becoming involved, as well as a consequence of having been highly involved in a task.

Conceptualizing Involvement

Considerations of the experience of involvement led us to look at the literatures of education, linguistics, communication, and psychology. Most useful to our early work was Tannen's (1985) description of discourse involvement. She proposed that when partners in discourse both agree on the intent of a message or a meta-message, they become more involved in an interaction than if they disagree about the intent of either message or meta-message. For example, if one party in a mediation believes the other is only making a show of trying to resolve a problem, they are less likely to be highly involved in the mediation conversation than if both of them believe the other is honestly attempting to resolve a problem. Although Tannen's ideas about discourse involvement have mostly been applied to the analysis of face-to-face conversations, they can apply as well to all types of discourse interactions including reading and writing, participating in online computer-mediated "conversations," or even preparing for oral discourse as in writing a speech.

In our previous research (Reed & Schallert, 1993), we found two dimensions of involvement, concentration and comprehension that are required for involvement in academic tasks regardless of whether the task is reading for a class, writing class papers, studying for tests, or listening to class lectures. Students reported that the experience of being involved occurred when they were able to concentrate deeply and to understand both the task and its content. These two dimensions of involvement are what we believe guide whether someone becomes involved, the level of a person's involvement, the length of involvement, and the reported experience of involvement after one is no longer involved.

Our subsequent research on college students' approaches to their academic discourse tasks (Reed et al., 1996) led us to appreciate the dynamic nature of involvement as a process. We found the following about involvement:

1. It waxes and wanes over time.
2. It wholly absorbs a person to the exclusion of simultaneous affect, motivations, emotions, or metacognitive thoughts.
3. It is generally (but not always) reported afterward as a positive, satisfying experience and is therefore itself motivational.
4. It has antecedents such as interest, concomitants such as a lack of awareness of time, and consequences such as an affinity for the involving task.
5. It occurs when there is a balance between appropriate level of difficulty of a task and ability of the participant at that task (Csikszentmihalyi, 1990).
6. It is difficult to measure while a person is actually involved.

In our research as well as in our reading of others' work, we have become acutely aware of the problems and special issues of measuring a phenomenon that waxes and wanes, sometimes momentarily, and never happens when one is consciously aware of it. In the next section, we discuss some of the problems and solutions associated with measuring involvement.

METHODOLOGICAL ISSUES IN STUDYING INVOLVEMENT

As might be expected, it is not easy to measure such a "slippery" intrapsychological construct as involvement. In our review of the literature, we have found several promising approaches. Csikszentmihalyi and Larson (1987) pioneered the Experience Sampling Method (ESM) in which participants wear beepers, and upon being randomly summoned, complete questionnaires about their current psychological states.

The advantage of this method is that one can be certain that individuals are being asked to respond immediately after something has happened. By saying immediately after, we are acknowledging that if a participant is beeped, his or her attention is suddenly turned to answering the questions and therefore is disengaged from the experience that was ongoing just prior to the beep. In other words, one is not immersed in both responding to the beep and in the prior activity. ESM is a clever way to ensure that participants have an experience contiguous with answering questions about that experience. Also, this method can provide a truly random sampling of time and activities that participants might not recall if responding to retrospective questions.

Another way to study involvement is to ask participants to recall experiences that were more or less involving. Reed and Schallert (1993) and Reed, Hagen, Wicker, and Schallert (1996) used this method both when interviewing students about academic tasks that might be on the continuum of involvement, and when asking students how involved they were during different phases of writing a paper or studying for an exam. One strength of this method is that students seem to find it easy to recall involving and uninvolving situations. Also, they seem quite capable of recalling how they responded to a task at different points in its progression. In the Reed et al. (1996) study, we were able to address the concern of whether participants would be able to recall and retrospectively evaluate their levels of involvement in a task. Comparisons of concurrent and retrospective reports indicated that remembering one's levels of involvement and affect within one week of the experience yielded similar data to those obtained during an ongoing task.

Other methodological approaches that we have tried did not prove to be as worthwhile. Schallert, Reed, and Goetz (1992) proposed that a secondary task paradigm could be effective. If participants were reading texts from a computer terminal and randomly given beeps to which to respond, those who were most involved would be slower to hit the spacebar in response to the beeps. We were not as successful as we had hoped with this technique, however. One reason, we hypothesized, is that our participants came to consider the beep task as the primary one, precluding their involvement in the text they were reading. Second, it is difficult to choose one text that could predictably be involving to most or all participants. Third, it might be the case that true task involvement, or the experience of "falling" into a task, may take more time than participants who are simply fulfilling a course requirement may be willing to give us. Participants in our latest study (Reed, Schallert, & Deithloff, 2000) reported that they needed to set aside enough time for a writing project in to experience involvement.

In light of these methodological issues, our own studies of involvement can be characterized as meshing qualitative and quantitative approaches. In our first studies (Reed & Schallert, 1993), we interviewed students about their involvement experiences in academic discourse tasks. These interview data were used to construct questionnaires that were analyzed with multidimensional scaling. We then corroborated our dimensional findings from that analysis with a quantitative study of phases of involvement over time in a specific writing task. In another study (Reed et al., 1996), we asked participants to complete questionnaires several times over a semester. We asked open-ended questions about their involvement, motivation, volition, and affect each time. In addition, we had participants rate their levels of involvement. This mix of qualitative, open-ended, experiential responses with more quantitative ratings helped us to understand involvement as a process that is dynamic and changes over the course of a task or even of a semester.

THE INTERFACE BETWEEN INVOLVEMENT AND SELF-REGULATION

Because we were studying involvement itself, the process as it unfolds, we noticed that it often took a characteristic pattern over time. For example, at the beginning of a writing task, students reported little to no involvement. However, under conditions that would promote involvement, such as optimal writer-task match, students reported progressing to high levels of involvement while in the midst of writing. Predictably, students told us that their levels of involvement fell off toward the end of their session of writing, sometimes abruptly as when an interruption occurred or more gradually as they found themselves losing interest and deciding to take a break (Reed & Schallert, 1993). This pattern to the process of involvement led us to be interested in its phases, what might be happening just before an involvement state, what might characterize the experience itself, and what might be its outcomes as the involved state recedes. We called these phases the antecedents, concomitants, and consequences of involvement.

One intriguing aspect of the antecedents to involvement was the frequency with which students reported using strategies to force themselves into becoming involved. Although some students slid effortlessly into involvement, more students needed to exercise strong volitional control (Reed, Schallert, & Deithloff, 2000). Thus, we came to see that involvement and self-regulation could work in concert in that these two may represent different steps in the psychological processes undertaken as one accomplishes a task. It is interesting to consider how self-regulation might influence and be influenced by the state of psychological engrossment. First, when individuals are deeply involved in a task, they are not employing metacognitive activities or experiencing emotional awareness. However, our previous research (Reed et al., 1996; Reed & Schallert, 1993), corroborated by that of others (Csikszentmihalyi, 1975, 1990; Turner et al., 1998), suggests that a *consequence* of having been involved in a task is engaging in metacognitive activity aimed toward recreating involvement because of the positive affect that arises when reflecting back on the involved experience.

Second, involvement seems to happen often because of self-regulated activity via volitional control strategies. Corno (1993) described volitional control strategies as those that carry learners across the divide of merely having a goal and actually doing the task. For example, a student who does not want to begin a research report can think about how good he or she will feel after beginning to locate all of the references needed. This is a positive volitional strategy. By contrast, a negative strategy would be predicting the negative consequences of not studying for a midterm exam. Schallert, Reed, Turner, and McCann (1997) found that use of volitional strategies such as thinking about negative consequences of doing poorly, or telling oneself that it is possible to succeed, vary over the course of a semester and are related to involvement and engagement.

In our most recent study of three semesters of a graduate writing course, we found that virtually all of the students reported using volitional strategies to get themselves into a state of involvement, as opposed to merely using these strategies to finish the task. The top five strategies mentioned were as follows: (a) limiting distractions and minimizing interference from other tasks; (b) making sure one is well-rested, psychologically and physically ready to undertake the task; (c) having a specific plan and sketching out ideas before writing; (d) engaging in brainstorming and free writing; and (e) talking with the intended audience for the piece in advance of writing.

Finally, one of the aspects of involvement in academic tasks that we have come to appreciate is the influence of timing on how students feel about their learning, their motivation, and their ability actually to complete a task. This dynamic change over the course of activities is something that is recreated at the level of the student's career most broadly, at the level of the semester, and then for each assignment. In terms of the experience of involvement, the deep attentional state we associate with involvement does not usually happen in an instant. It takes time for involvement to take over and there is a sense of going into and out of the experience of involvement. The data we most recently gathered allowed us to see for the first time that self-regulation, a metacognitive activity that we had not previously connected to involvement, is critical in helping an individual enter into involvement or regain it if it has been lost. In other words, a person may be riding a wave of deep involvement that then crashes or is interrupted, leading to metacognitive awareness that then invokes strategies to renew involvement, and so on.

STUDYING PHASES OF A TASK TO UNDERSTAND PROCESSES

Our contribution to the self-regulation literature arises from our unique qualitative approach that allowed us to capture the phase change in a task where self-regulatory processes disappear and a new, non-self-focused state takes over. By changing the perspective taken on processes comprising academic tasks, we broaden our understanding of the whole learning process. When looking at involvement, self-regulation becomes a precursor; when focusing on self-regulation, involvement becomes its consequence, one possible outcome, result, or reward for the self-regulatory activity.

Thus, the advantage of our approach is that we can observe the distinct phases of a task and thereby see the role self-regulation can play in concert with other processes. For example, the four questionnaires in our most recent study were administered and completed at spaced intervals over a semester. These questionnaires were comprised of structured but open-ended probes that allowed our participants freedom to provide their insights about their own experiences. The first questionnaire began with general questions such as "What is writing?" and even as it broached the topic of involvement with a question such as "Give reasons for your level of involvement," remained open-ended. We used the students' responses to the first questionnaire to construct probes for the second, and so on for the third and fourth questionnaires. Each questionnaire began with more general questions before becoming more focused. For example, in answer to the question "What are your top strategies for getting yourself involved in your writing?" (Questionnaire #3), students wrote, "I get alone in a library or a place with very limited distractions," "I make sure I am physically and psychologically ready," and "I begin with or switch to an easy section."

Had we used a more quantitative approach, a questionnaire with stricter response limitations, the students' conceptions of what we were asking about might have interfered with their ability to respond to our questions. Our open-ended questions encouraged the students to provide more varied and subtle responses thus allowing us to develop a richer representation of involvement. At the same time, our conceptions of involvement as a phased process led us to ask students questions that they answered by pointing to self-regulatory processes. Having set out to study a process that we had conceptualized to be devoid of metacognitive controls, we were surprised to encounter in our participants' responses such clear allusions to the role self-regulation plays in involvement.

CONCLUSION

We want to conclude by describing the major insights we gained by using qualitative methods to study self-regulation and involvement. We realized firsthand some of the differences between qualitative and quantitative approaches to research. As Eisner (1998) mentioned, studies are qualitative and quantitative by degree. A major characteristic of quantitative research is the focus on variables that a researcher predicts are related to a dependent variable. Conversely, qualitative research has an "interpretive character" (Eisner, 1998) with the goal of describing subjective experiences. In fact, qualitative studies open the possibility of learning about variables the researcher did not even expect *a priori*. This is exactly what happened to us over the course of our work on involvement.

Our quantitative studies allowed us to come to some interesting insights about the general process of involvement. For example, we concluded that involvement was comprised of two dimensions, concentration and comprehension, and that the level of involvement seemed to be significantly greater in the midst of tasks than it was at the beginnings and ends of those tasks. We asked about and learned that involvement was inversely related to both positive and negative affect. Thus, our more quantitative approaches taught us about the interrelationships of variables or the "shape" of the involvement process as it ebbs and flows during a time period. By contrast, our qualitative studies taught us more about participants' intrasubjective experience of being involved. In particular, we came to appreciate the role of self-regulation in undertaking an academic task and how it may engender involvement. In the beginning of our research program, we did not consider self-regulation to be at all related to involvement. In fact, we did not ask our participants any questions that would have allowed them to reveal the connection between self-regulatory activities and involvement. However, when presented with open-ended, qualitative questionnaires that did not restrict their responses, our participants told us quite clearly that self-regulative volitional strategies play a major role in helping them become involved. Even though our quantitative research suggested that being in the midst of involvement precluded any competing cognitions especially those related to worrying about staying on task, we are now convinced that many kinds of cognitive and motivational variables play a role in a process marked by an involvement phase. Qualitative and quantitative methods seem complementary and allow for the triangulation of interpretations needed to provide for a fuller vision of psychological phenomena.

REFERENCES

Corno, L. (1993). The best-laid plans: Modern conceptions of volition and educational research. *Educational Researcher, 22*(2), 14–22.

Csikszentmihalyi, M. (1975). *Beyond boredom and anxiety.* San Francisco: Jossey-Bass.

Csikszentmihalyi, M. (1990). *Flow: The psychology of optimal experience.* New York: HarperCollins.

Csikszentmihalyi, M., & Larson, R. (1987). Validity and reliability of the experience-sampling method. *The Journal of Nervous and Mental Disease, 175,* 526–536.

Eisner, E. W. (1998). *The enlightened eye: Qualitative inquiry and the enhancement of educational practice.* Upper Saddle River, NJ: Prentice-Hall.

Guthrie, J., & Wigfield, A. (1997). Reading engagement: A rationale for theory and teaching. In J. Guthrie & A. Wigfield (Eds.), *Promoting literacy through integrated teaching* (pp. 1–12). Chicago: International Reading Association.

Guthrie, J. T., Van Meter, P., McCann, A. D., Wigfield, A., Bennett, L., Poundstone, C. C., et al. (1996). Growth of literacy engagement: Changes in motivations and strategies during concept-oriented reading instruction. *Reading Research Quarterly, 31,* 306–332.

Krapp, A., Hidi, S., & Renninger, K. A. (1992). Interest, learning and development. In K. A. Renninger, S. Hidi, & A. Krapp (Eds.), *The role of interest in learning and development* (pp. 3–26). Hillsdale, NJ: Lawrence Erlbaum Associates, Inc.

Reed, J. H., Hagen, A. S., Wicker, F. W., & Schallert, D. L. (1996). Involvement as a temporal dynamic: Affective factors in studying for exams. *Journal of Educational Psychology, 88,* 101–109.

Reed, J. H., & Schallert, D. L. (1993). Discourse involvement: An exploration of a cognitive/motivational construct in academic discourse tasks. *Journal of Educational Psychology, 85,* 253–266.

Reed, J. H., Schallert, D. L., & Deithloff, L. (2000, April). *Understanding students' involvement in academic tasks.* Paper presented at the American Educational Research Association meeting, New Orleans, LA.

Schallert, D. L., & Reed, J. H. (1997). The pull of the text and the process of involvement in one's reading. In J. Guthrie & A. Wigfield (Eds.), *Promoting literacy through integrated teaching* (pp. 68–85). Chicago: International Reading Association.

Schallert, D. L., Reed, J. H., & Goetz, E. T. (1992, December). *Involvement in a reading task and its relationship to comprehensibility and interestingness: Exploring interrelationships and validating a measure of involvement.* Paper presented at the National Reading Conference, San Antonio, TX.

Schallert, D. L., Reed, J. H., Turner, J. E., & McCann, E. J. (1997, April). *Engagement in long-term academic tasks: The fluctuating, complementary role of involvement and volition.* Paper presented at the annual meeting of the American Educational Research Association, Chicago.

Tannen, D. (1985). Relative focus on involvement in oral and written discourse. In D. R. Olson (Ed.), *Literacy, language, and learning: The nature and consequences of reading and writing.* London: Cambridge University Press.

Turner, J. C., Meyer, D. K, Cox, K. E., Logan, C., DiCintio, M., & Thomas, C. T. (1998). Creating contexts for involvement in mathematics. *Journal of Educational Psychology, 90,* 730–745.

Zimmerman, B. J. (1990). Self-regulated learning and academic achievement: An overview. *Educational Psychologist, 21,* 3–18.

EDUCATIONAL PSYCHOLOGIST, *37*(1), 59–63

Qualitative Approaches to Investigating Self-Regulated Learning: Contributions and Challenges

Deborah L. Butler
Department of Educational and Counseling Psychology and Special Education
University of British Columbia

The articles included in this special issue demonstrate how qualitative methodologies can be profitably employed to enhance understanding related to self-regulated learning (SRL) and the contexts that support it. This concluding discussion underlines ways in which these articles contribute to an understanding of SRL, with a particular focus on the advantages associated with the methodologies employed. Discussion centers on 4 themes that emerged across articles from authors' attempts to view SRL from a qualitative perspective. These themes include consideration of (a) how SRL should be defined, (b) investigating SRL in context, (c) documenting intervention–outcome linkages, and (d) the interplay between researchers', teachers', and students' co-constructions of theories of SRL. As part of the discussion in each section, the article highlights outstanding conceptual and methodological challenges for researchers and educators interested in SRL.

The articles in this special issue paint a broad and complex portrait of self-regulated learning (SRL) as it appears and develops across contexts and over time. Taken together, the articles demonstrate how qualitative methodologies can be employed profitably to address a range of research questions with learners at different ages. For example, across articles, the focus of study ranges from a fine-grained analysis of intrapsychological experience (Reed, Schallert, & Deithloff 2001), to studies of how classroom discourse and practices support self-regulated performance in literacy, math, or science (Meyer & Turner, 2001; Patrick & Middleton, 2001; Perry, VandeKamp, Mercer, & Nordby, 2001), to a study of the impact on SRL of the broader school culture (De Groot, 2001). Collectively, the articles investigate SRL across the life span, with descriptions of primary classrooms that support SRL, instruction that fosters SRL by students in Grades 5 to 8 (Meyer & Turner, 2001; Patrick & Middleton, 2001), adolescents' perspectives on school culture and its relationship to learning (De Groot), and SRL's association with immersion in learning by college-level and post-graduate students (Reed et al., 2001).

Within each article, authors make a unique contribution to understanding SRL and the contexts that support its development. Nonetheless, four important themes can be identified across papers that will form the basis for discussion here. These themes emerge from the attempt by authors to view SRL from a qualitative perspective and include consideration of (a) the definition of SRL, (b) the investigation of SRL in context, (c) the documentation of intervention–outcome linkages, and (d) the interplay between researchers', teachers', and students' co-constructions of theories of SRL. Upcoming sections define contributions made by authors in each area and surface outstanding conceptual and methodological challenges.

Requests for reprints should be sent to Deborah L. Butler, Department of Educational and Counseling Psychology and Special Education, University of British Columbia, 2125 Main Mall, Vancouver, BC, Canada V6T 1Z4. E-mail: deborah.butler@ubc.ca

DEFINING SRL

Over the past 30 years, definitions of SRL have become increasingly encompassing (Paris & Paris, 2001). Early descriptions characterized self-regulated learners as metacognitively aware, planful, and strategic (Brown, 1987; Butler, 1998b; Flavell, 1976). Subsequently, through the 1980s and 1990s, conceptions of SRL evolved to comprise interactions between students' knowledge (e.g., metacognitive, domain specific, epistemological), metacognitive skill (e.g., planning, monitoring), motivation (e.g., self-efficacy beliefs, attributions), and cognition (e.g., application of a cognitive strategy; Alexander & Judy, 1988; Borkowski & Muthukrishna, 1992; Butler, 1998b; Butler & Winne, 1995; Schommer, 1990; Schunk, 1994). An emphasis has been on how SRL is a function of the knowledge and skill that students construct over time (Paris & Byrnes, 1989).

At the same time, evolving definitions of SRL focus on how enactment of self-regulated approaches to learning depends on *individuals* acting in *social* contexts (e.g., Paris & Paris, 2001; Patrick & Middleton, 2001; Zimmerman, 1995). This perspective emphasizes that self-regulated learning emerges from more than just individual knowledge and skill. Rather, self-regulation also "involves a social aspect that includes interactions with peers and teachers" (Patrick & Middleton, 2001) who shape students' task engagement by "co-regulating" learning (Meyer & Turner, 2001). By definition, self-regulated learning is now thought to occur when students are motivated to reflectively and strategically engage in learning activities within environments that foster self-regulation.

In line with emerging definitions of SRL, in this special issue, authors investigate the interplay between motivation, affect, cognitive strategies, metacognition, and social contexts as they shape students' approaches to learning. Indeed, one of the most significant contributions of this set of articles is definition of methodological approaches that successfully capture the interactions among variables that have most often been investigated in a more piecemeal fashion. An excellent example is Patrick and Middleton's (2001) combined use of observations and interviews to document how students were "engaged cognitively, metacognitively, motivationally, or collaboratively" in project-based science. In general, qualitative approaches that investigate the recursive interactions between constructs advance understanding of how SRL can be supported in naturalistic contexts and in real time (Perry et al., 2001). Further, unlike aggregated measures of SRL that describe students' learning across contexts or tasks (Winne & Perry, 2000), qualitative methods allow researchers to complete more fine-grained analyses of instances of SRL as they play out in context. In Winne and Perry's (2000) terms, qualitative methods support researchers' attempts to investigate SRL as an "event" (p. 534).

The complex definitions of SRL that have evolved over the past 30 years can be linked to shifts in methodology (Paris & Paris, 2001). As Patrick and Middleton (2001) explain, sociocultural perspectives that emphasize how SRL is shaped socially have led to qualitative methodologies that investigate SRL in context (see also Perry et al., 2001). As a result, emerging definitions of SRL have assisted researchers and teachers to develop integrative theories about learning that are broadly encompassing. However, definitions of SRL that include both social and individual processes also raise important conceptual questions. For example, *how* is SRL both an individual and a social process? What are individual and sociocultural influences on students' development of SRL (Butler, 1998a)? Increased clarity on these topics may be useful in building theory, constructing methodologies for studying SRL, and advancing practice.

For example, the articles in this special issue document how students' enactment of SRL is not just a function of what an individual brings to the learning context. Students' self-regulation can be enhanced, or inhibited, by the circumstances in which they find themselves. At a simple level, whether or not students self-regulate depends on whether or not they are afforded opportunities to do so (e.g., choice, control, opportunities for self-appraisal; Perry et al., 2001). An important implication is that it is not possible to judge individuals' capacity to self-regulate without consideration of context. Note, for example, Perry's (1998) finding that even young children are capable of self-regulating in supportive settings.

At a more subtle level, definitions of SRL as socially influenced recognize that students' regulation of learning can be guided by others (i.e., co-regulation of learning supported using classroom discourse, supportive materials, procedural facilitators, etc.). Indeed, another significant contribution of the articles in this special issue is the demonstration of how qualitative methods can capture the way in which co-regulation operates and can be faded as students take more responsibility for learning (e.g., Meyer & Turner, 2001). These findings clearly document that the process by which SRL develops is, at least in part, a social one.

But does this mean that SRL, per se, is a social process? Or, could SRL be the endpoint of a process of development? Certainly, few educators would be satisfied with students' continuous reliance on others to solve math problems, even if social support is instrumental in promoting students' development of SRL. Indeed, most definitions of SRL have at their core the goal of students' self-directing learning independently. For example, Paris and Paris (2001) link self-regulation to "autonomy and control by the individual who monitors, directs, and regulates action toward goals of information acquisition, expanding expertise, and self-improvement" (Paris & Paris, p. 89). Even Meyer and Turner (2001) who explicitly describe SRL as a social process, identify students' development of autonomy and responsibility as important instructional goals. If SRL is a social process, where do constructs such as independence, control, autonomy, and responsibility fit in? Further, what are individual contributions to SRL development (see Butler, 1998a; Butler & Winne, 1995)? Although integrative and beneficial in numerous respects, broad definitions of SRL that encompass a large variety of individual and social processes may obscure important distinctions.

INVESTIGATING SRL IN CONTEXT

Yin (1994) argued that an optimal time to use qualitative methods is when it is not possible to separate a phenomenon from its context. It could be argued that understanding SRL and supportive contexts presents just such an occasion. Consider, for example, attempts to study the features of instrumental, or "scaffolded," instruction that support self-regulation (e.g., Meyer & Turner, 2001). Researchers have struggled to construct coding schemes that define teacher acts (e.g.., open vs. closed questions) as instances of "scaffolded" rather than "nonscaffolded" instruction. However, as Meyer and Turner acknowledge, even the most teacher-directed (apparently nonscaffolded) statement could be an instance of instrumental support if it serves to support self-regulation (e.g., self-appraisal). The problem is that whether or not a given act is instrumental depends on how that act functions in context, given a history of interaction. Similarly, when investigating SRL, Butler (1998b) described how a given student action (e.g., paraphrasing while reading) could be classed as a cognitive (e.g., comprehension building) or metacognitive (e.g., self-regulating) strategy, depending on the purpose the activity served. Thus, an opportunity, and challenge, for researchers is to define coding schemes based on the function of events in context, rather than on the surface features of teacher or student activities. Similarly, the challenge for researchers developing survey measures of SRL (Winne & Perry, 2000) is to preserve the meaning of events across individuals and out of context.

While adopting a qualitative "lens" (Patrick & Middleton, 2001), the researchers writing for this special issue were able to demonstrate how multiple methods can be employed in tandem to uncover the interplay between the social and individual processes that shape SRL in context and "on-line." For example, interviews were used to uncover individuals' perspectives in relation to particular events, thereby providing a window into the types of beliefs, knowledge, and skills that shape approaches to learning (e.g., De Groot, 2001; Meyer & Turner, 2001). At the same time, observations documented social interactions to suggest the meaning of events in context (e.g., Meyer & Turner, 2001; Perry et al., 2001).

Adopting a qualitative lens and multiple methods for investigating SRL also enabled the researchers to challenge SRL theories derived using other methods. Although the research tools employed by authors (e.g., research questions, coding schemes) were clearly shaped by existing theory, the techniques allowed researchers to build theory inductively and to critique extant assumptions (Merriam, 1998). For example, examining SRL in context led Perry (1998) to question whether young children are not capable of self-regulation. Similarly, Patrick and Middleton (2001) provided data that challenges the validity of survey instruments used to evaluate SRL. Inconsistencies between ratings given to surveys and what students actually did led Patrick and Middleton to suggest either that researchers and students do not interpret survey questions in the same way, or that researchers have been asking the wrong research questions. Such discrepant findings, uncovered using multiple methods that juxtapose aggregated perceptions with actions observed in context, can be extremely useful to developers of survey instruments, who can "bootstrap" (Winne & Perry, 2000) from qualitative findings to develop better theories and measures of SRL.

Reed et al. (2001) make a unique contribution to understanding SRL as an event by examining the relationship between SRL and "involvement." According to Reed et al., involvement describes a special type of task engagement during which a learner is wholly concentrated on a given task with deep comprehension of the material, similar to the "flow" state described by Csikszentmihalyi (1990). Further, they suggest that the consciously mediated and reflective processing characteristic of SRL can serve as either a precursor to or consequence of involvement. For example, when students employ volition control strategies to minimize distractions and focus attention, they set up the conditions necessary to establish a state of involvement (Reed et al., 2001). In this respect, Reed et al.'s study of involvement contributes to an understanding of where and how SRL fits into student learning and task engagement. The methodologies Reed et al. employ (interviews and event sampling) are designed to describe the boundaries between involvement and SRL as learning sequences unfold.

Methodologically, Reed et al. demonstrate the difficulty inherent in documenting an event that is, by definition, dissolved once it comes under conscious reflection. Their study raises an interesting question regarding how researchers can access cognitive processes that are not consciously mediated (especially using interpretive methods, which often rely on individuals' ability to consciously report on experience). This methodological problem also is a barrier to understanding the potential role of automatic processing in SRL. Although the hallmark of SRL is considered to be students' active and reflective regulation of their learning processes, questions can be raised regarding how much "self-regulation" transpires outside of direct awareness (Butler, 1998b). For example, is comprehension monitoring in reading always consciously mediated? When and how does awareness of a comprehension breakdown emerge? Additional research could examine what it is that triggers students to make the transition between episodes of involvement and self-regulation. Perhaps combinations of event sampling, observations, "traces," and interviews can contribute to understanding the interplay between consciously- and non-consciously mediated learning activities (Winne & Perry, 2000).

DOCUMENTING INTERVENTION–OUTCOME LINKAGES

Several articles in this special issue examine linkages between learning environments and outcomes related to SRL. A strength of the qualitative methods employed is that they explicitly document the connection between interventions and outcomes, thereby bolstering internal validity (Creswell, 1998). For example, in a sequence of studies, Perry and her colleagues (see Perry et al., 2001) observed students and teachers in classrooms, intervened with teachers interested in revising instructional practices, and then documented both shifts in teachers' practice and corresponding outcomes for students. This comprehensive strategy allowed her to demonstrate not only that features of classroom environments could be associated with greater self-regulation (correlational data afforded by the initial classroom observations), but also that making shifts in instructional practice had direct effects on student learning (supporting causal inferences). Another example is provided by De Groot (2001). In one of her studies, classroom organization and school culture were altered for students in Grades 7 and 8. By interviewing students at multiple points in time across three grade levels, De Groot was able to associate changes in students' perceptions with shifts in school organizational structure across time. At a more microlevel, Meyer and Turner's (2001) discourse analysis documents the process of co-regulation in relation to students' increasing assumption of responsibility for their own learning (i.e., self-regulation). Taken together, these articles illustrate the benefits of using qualitative methods for advancing theoretical understanding regarding organizational, instructional, and classroom practices that support SRL. Thick, rich descriptions of instruction–outcome linkages are also useful for communicating research findings because they allow practitioners to vicariously witness complex processes in context, thereby supporting naturalistic generalization, or "case to case" transfer (Lincoln & Guba, 1985; Merriam, 1998).

When faced with the mass of data typically collected in qualitative studies, researchers are forced to be selective in terms of data they analyze and report. The articles included in this special issue illustrate some of the choices that qualitative researchers might make in terms of documenting intervention–outcome linkages, each of which has benefits and limitations. For example, one strategy for presenting findings is to select one or more ideal cases to describe in depth (e.g., Perry et al., 2001). This strategy is especially useful for illustrating how interventions *can* work. Further, detailed descriptions of constructive classroom practices provide guidance for educators interested in establishing similar practices themselves. Potential pitfalls with this approach, however, include overreliance on a single case (or type of case) when building theory, or an overly optimistic presentation of how classroom environments can be structured to support SRL. Equally interesting, for example, would be a report from Perry's research program describing what transpired for teachers who were not as successful in shifting their practices. Documenting the experience of unsuccessful teachers would provide important information regarding barriers or challenges that practitioners might face.

Another example of a reporting strategy is to illuminate a phenomenon by drawing stark contrasts. Using this strategy, researchers might describe extreme cases on some dimension, such as instructional discourse that is scaffolded or nonscaffolded (e.g., Meyer & Turner, 2001). This approach can be very helpful in terms of defining or conceptualizing constructs. A danger, however, is that the muddiness of "reality" may not be adequately represented in the extremes, so that distinctions that seem clear in "theory" have less relevance in practice. A final example of a potential presentation strategy would be to describe what happened across cases or events more comprehensively (e.g., De Groot, 2001). This approach demands an accounting not only of what might be "generally" true across cases, but also a sense of the variability in responses. One advantage of this approach is that it provides an overview of both typical and discrepant findings. A thorough reporting of results is also likely to appeal most to researchers looking for a comprehensive treatment of evidence.

In general, a recommendation for constructing any qualitative report is to avoid presenting only positive evidence for generalized conclusions, while skirting discussion of disconfirming evidence and discrepant findings. Although some qualitative researchers caution against generalizing from qualitative studies in the first place (e.g., Lincoln & Guba, 1985), most acknowledge that there is a role for qualitative methods in both generating and testing theory (e.g., Merriam, 1998; Yin, 1994). In the articles included in this special issue, the authors clearly wish not just to document and describe specific instances of SRL, but also to draw theoretical conclusions about the relationships between important variables as they interact in context. To warrant generalized conclusions about what is true of SRL and contexts that support it, it is important for researchers to indicate how relevant evidence was treated comprehensively and disconfirming evidence was considered. One strategy for documenting both common themes and discrepant findings is to provide a matrix or display that presents general trends in tandem with evidence that illustrates particular points (e.g., Butler, Novak, Beckingham, Jarvis, & Elaschuk, 2001; Miles & Huberman, 1994). At a minimum, to establish credibility, it is essential that researchers explicate how methodological decisions are logically connected to research purposes and warrant conclusions, particularly generalizations (Creswell, 1998; Merriam, 1998; Miles & Huberman, 1994).

CONSTRUCTING THEORIES ABOUT TEACHING AND LEARNING

Paris and Paris (2001) suggested that students construct theories about SRL as they are engaged in academic activities. This suggestion is consistent with research findings showing that students construct understandings about tasks and learning that reflect the work they are assigned, for better or for worse (Butler, 1998b; Campione, Brown, & O'Connell, 1988; Paris & Byrnes, 1989). The papers in this special issue document how classroom tasks and instructional discourse can support students' construction of knowledge and beliefs that support, rather than undermine, self-regulation (Borkowski & Muthukrishna, 1992).

Although the articles presented in this special issue focus on students' construction of theories of SRL, they also show how teachers and researchers are actively engaged in constructing understandings about SRL that drive their teaching or research activities. Consider that the focus of this special issue is on strategies for advancing theories of SRL held by researchers (using qualitative methodological tools). Less obvious, perhaps, is the parallel effort by researchers to support teachers' construction of theories related to SRL in order to shape their instructional decision making. Perry et al.'s article provides an excellent example of a research program that dovetails professional development activities founded on a model of SRL (i.e., promoting reflective and strategic decision making in practice) with the development of classroom practices that support SRL in students. A similar, multilayered effort is apparent in the work of Butler and her colleagues (see Butler et al., 2001). A profitable area for further research could center on strategies for engaging collaborative teams of researchers, teachers, and students in co-constructing theories of SRL.

CONCLUSION

Recently, Winne and Perry (2000) provided an insightful analysis of methodological approaches used to measure self-regulated learning (SRL). At the end of their chapter, they call for additional fine-tuning of methodological approaches in three areas. These were, first, to find strategies for investigating SRL as an "event," that is as it unfolds in real time within particular contexts; second, to employ methodological triangulation, wherein multiple methods are used to give a more complex and complete picture of interacting SRL processes and the contexts in which they occur; and third, to investigate SRL across the age spectrum, as it plays out from childhood through to adulthood. Taken together, the five papers included in this special issue make contributions in each of these areas. Thus, a major focus of this concluding article has been to highlight the articles' contributions in terms both of understanding SRL and of identifying methodological tools for enhancing SRL research. At the same time, I have attempted to uncover a sampling of the conceptual and methodological challenges that remain and to suggest possible strategies for addressing them.

REFERENCES

Alexander, P. A., & Judy, J. E. (1988). The interaction of domain-specific and strategic knowledge in academic performance. *Review of Educational Research, 58,* 375–404.

Borkowski, J. G., & Muthukrishna, N. (1992). Moving metacognition into the classroom: "Working models" and effective strategy teaching. In M. Pressley, K. R. Harris, & J. T. Guthrie (Eds.), *Promoting academic competence and literacy in school* (pp. 477–501). Toronto, Canada: Academic.

Brown, A. L. (1987). Metacognition, executive control, self-regulation, and other more mysterious mechanisms. In F. E. Weinert & R. H. Kluwe (Eds.), *Metacognition, Motivation, and Understanding* (pp. 65–116). Hillsdale, NJ: Lawrence Erlbaum Associates, Inc.

Butler, D. L. (1998a). In search of the architect of learning: A commentary on scaffolding as a metaphor for instructional interactions. *Journal of Learning Disabilities, 31*(4), 374–385.

Butler, D. L. (1998b). Metacognition and learning disabilities. In B. Y. L. Wong (Ed.), *Learning about learning disabilities* (2nd ed., pp. 277–307). Toronto, Canada: Academic.

Butler, D. L., Novak, H., Beckingham, B., Jarvis, S., & Elaschuk, C. L. (2001, April). *Professional development and meaningful change: Towards sustaining an instructional innovation.* Presented at the annual meeting of the American Educational Research Association, Seattle, WA.

Butler, D.L., & Winne, P.H. (1995). Feedback and self-regulated learning: A theoretical synthesis. *Review of Educational Research, 65,* 245–281.

Campione, J. C., Brown, A. L., & O'Connell, M. L. (1988). Metacognition: On the importance of understanding what you are doing. In R. I. Charles & E. A. Silver (Eds.), *The teaching and assessing of mathematical problem solving* (Vol. 3, pp. 93–114). Hillsdale, NJ: Lawrence Erlbaum Associates, Inc.

Creswell, J. W. (1998). *Qualitative inquiry and research design: Choosing among five traditions.* Thousand Oaks, CA: Sage.

Csikzentmihalyi, M. (1990). *Flow: The psychology of optimal experience.* New York: HarperCollins.

De Groot, E. V. (2002). Learning through interviewing: Students and teachers talk about learning and schooling. *Educational Psychologist, 37,* 47–58.

Flavell, J. H. (1976). Metacognitive aspects of problem solving. In L. B. Resnick (Ed.), *The nature of intelligence* (pp. 231–235). Hillsdale, NJ: Lawrence Erlbaum Associates, Inc.

Lincoln, Y. S., & Guba, E. G. (1985). *Naturalistic inquiry.* Newbury Park, CA: Sage.

Merriam, S. B. (1998). *Qualitative research and case study applications in education.* San Francisco: Jossey-Bass.

Meyer, D. K., & Turner, J. C. (2002). Using instructional discourse analysis to study the scaffolding of student self-regulation. *Educational Psychologist, 37,* 5–13.

Miles, M. B., & Huberman, A. M. (1994). *Qualitative data analysis: An expanded sourcebook* (2nd ed.). Thousand Oaks, CA: Sage.

Paris, S. G., & Byrnes, J. P. (1989). The constructivist approach to self-regulation and learning in the classroom. In B. J. Zimmerman & D. H. Schunk (Eds.), *Self-regulated learning and academic achievement: Theory, research, and practice* (pp. 169–200). New York: Springer-Verlag.

Paris, S. G., & Paris, A. H. (2001). Classroom applications of research on self-regulated learning. *Educational Psychologist, 36*(2), 89–101.

Patrick, H., & Middleton, M. J. (2002). Turning the kaleidoscope: What we see when self-regulated learning is viewed with a qualitative lens. *Educational Psychologist, 37,* 27–39.

Perry, N. E. (1998). Young children's self-regulated learning and contexts that support it. *Journal of Educational Psychology, 90,* 715–729.

Perry, N. E., VandeKamp, K. O., Mercer, L. K., & Nordby, C. J. (2002). Investigating teacher-student interactions that foster self-regulated learning. *Educational Psychologist, 37,* 15–25.

Reed, J. H., Schallert, D. L., & Deithloff, L. F. (2002). Investigating the interface between self-regulation and involvement processes. *Educational Psychologist, 37,* 41–45.

Schommer, M. (1990). Effects of beliefs about the nature of knowledge on comprehension. *Journal of Educational Psychology, 82,* 498–504.

Schunk, D. H. (1994). Self-regulation of self-efficacy and attributions in academic settings. In D. H. Schunk & B. J. Zimmerman (Eds.), *Self-regulation of learning and performance: Issues and educational applications* (pp. 75–99). Hillsdale, NJ: Lawrence Erlbaum Associates, Inc.

Winne, P. H., & Perry, N. E. (2000). Measuring self-regulated learning. In P. Pintrich, M. Boekarts, & M. Zeidner (Eds.), *Handbook of Self-Regulation* (pp. 531–566). Orlando, FL: Academic.

Yin, R. K. (1994). *Case study research: Design and methods* (2nd ed.). Thousand Oaks, CA: Sage.

Zimmerman, B. J. (1995). Self-regulation involves more than metacognition: A social cognitive perspective. *Educational Psychologist, 30,* 217–221.

EDUCATIONAL PSYCHOLOGIST, *37*(1), 65

List of Reviewers for Volume 37, Number 1

The following list of individuals served as reviewers for this special issue on "Using Qualitative Methods to Enrich Understandings of Self-Regulated Learning." The editors and guest editor thank these reviewers for their conscientious service to the journal.

Patricia Alexander
Eric Anderman
Lynley Anderman
Phyllis Blumenfeld
John Freeman
Mary McCaslin
Kit Tisdale
Julie Turner
Philip Winne
Anita Woolfolk-Hoy

INSTRUCTIONS TO AUTHORS

STATEMENT OF PURPOSE

The *Educational Psychologist* publishes scholarly essays, reviews, critiques, and articles of a theoretical/conceptual nature that contribute to our understanding of the issues, problems, and research associated with the field of educational psychology. Articles representing all aspects of educational psychology are encouraged. This journal, however, does not publish articles whose primary purpose is to report the method and results of an empirical study.

SCREEN FOR APPROPRIATENESS

By submitting manuscripts to the *Educational Psychologist,* authors are confirming that the manuscripts have not been published and are not under consideration for publication elsewhere. Prior to submission, authors should determine whether their manuscripts correspond to the journal's statement of purpose—to publish essays, critiques, and articles of a theoretical/conceptual nature that contribute to our understanding of the issues, problems, and research associated with the field of educational psychology. Articles consistent with the journal's purpose include critical, integrative reviews of educational psychology research; conceptual or theoretical syntheses or analyses of educational psychology research; scientifically documented digests of educational psychology research relevant to policy issues; and documented, scholarly essays of general interest to the educational psychology community. Consistent with the journal's mission to serve as a forum for important ideas in educational psychology, articles of varying lengths and covering all aspects of educational psychology will be considered, including articles focusing on implications for educational theory, research, practice, or policy. Articles that report mainly the results of an empirical study (e.g., would be appropriate for the *Journal of Educational Psychology*) or articles that are intended mainly as practical guides (without research documentation) are inappropriate for the *EP* and will be returned to the authors. In addition to publishing regular articles, the journal publishes special issues that are devoted to important themes in educational psychology and keynote reviews with published peer commentary. Authors interested in the latter formats are requested to contact the editor prior to submitting a proposal for a special issue or keynote review.

SUBMISSION OF MANUSCRIPTS

Manuscripts must be prepared in accordance with the following instructions.

FOLLOW APA STYLE

Authors should follow the *Publication Manual of the American Psychological Association* (4th ed.) in preparing manuscripts for submission to this journal. All manuscripts must be prefaced by an abstract of 100–150 words on a separate sheet. All manuscript pages, including reference lists and tables, must be typed double-spaced. All figures must be camera ready. Authors should comply with "Guidelines to Reduce Bias in Language" as printed in the *Publication Manual.* Manuscripts that fail to conform to APA-style guidelines will be returned to the author(s).

PREPARE FOR BLIND PEER REVIEW

All articles appearing in the *EP* are peer reviewed. Because the reviewers have agreed to participate in a blind reviewing system, authors submitting manuscripts are requested to include with each copy of the manuscript a cover sheet that shows the title of the manuscript, the names of the authors, the authors' institutional affiliations, the mailing address, the date the manuscript is submitted, and a running head. The first page of the manuscript should omit the authors' names and affiliations but should include the title of the manuscript and the date it is submitted. Footnotes containing information pertaining to the authors' identities or affiliations should be placed on separate pages. Every effort should be made by authors to see that the manuscript itself contains no clues to their identities.

FOLLOW COPYRIGHT LAWS

Authors are responsible for obtaining and providing written permission from copyright owners for reprinting previously published illustrations, tables, or lengthy quotes (500 or more words). Authors are responsible for the accuracy of the material in their manuscripts.

SUBMIT FIVE COPIES

Send five copies of your manuscripts (an original and four duplicates) to: Philip H. Winne and Lyn Corno, Coeditors, *Educational Psychologist,* Faculty of Education, Simon Fraser University, Burnaby, British Columbia, Canada V5A 1S6. Authors should keep a copy of the manuscript to guard against loss in the mail. After a manuscript is accepted for publication, its author is asked to provide a computer disk containing the manuscript file. Files are copyedited and typeset into page proofs. Authors read proofs to correct errors and answer editors' queries.